Comment on *The Other Side of the Wall:*

A brave, poignant, and invaluable exposure to ｡ ⎵ ⎵
endured by the Palestinian people living under a cruel occupation that has
lasted for fifty years with no end in sight.

Richard Hardigan is no spectator of this ordeal, writing as one who has for
some months stood shoulder-to-shoulder in solidarity with the Palestinians,
inspired by their extraordinary resolve, resilience, and above all by their loving
hospitality. Every American should be forced to read this illuminating book!

    —Professor Richard Falk, former UN Special Rapporteur on Palestine

Richard Hardigan . . . has written what we have been waiting for: a measured,
you-are-there account . . . a vivid journal that takes us past slogans and ideol-
ogies.

    —Philip Weiss, co-founder and editor of *Mondoweiss*

The Other Side of the Wall is a wrenching and revealing account that can only
be conveyed by someone who has lived its exasperating and at times heartbreaking details. Richard Hardigan tells the story of the Israeli occupation of
Palestine with utmost integrity. It is a powerful experience . . . dauntingly real
and unapologetically honest. A strongly recommended read.

    —Ramzy Baroud,
        author *My Father was a Freedom Fighter* and *Searching Jenin*

. . . Richard Hardigan takes you onto the ground in occupied Palestine . . .
He conveys the message that, for the sake of our own humanity, we must
not avert our eyes and look away, but each in our own capacity must join in
solidarity with the oppressed.

    —Jeremy Hammond,
        author *Obstacle to Peace: The US Role in the Israeli-Palestinian*

In this informative and disturbing book, Richard Hardigan brings the reader into the stark, brutal reality of Palestinian suffering. From personal accounts of the suffering of people who quickly became close friends, to the biased reporting in the western media, the reader is brought face-to-face with the harsh truths of the Israeli occupation. A must-read for anyone wanting to be fully informed about this timely issue.

—Robert Fantina, author
Empire, Racism and Genocide: A History of US Foreign Policy

A searing first-person account. Hardigan describes the murder, theft, desecration and destruction regularly visited on Palestinians by their Israeli tormentors . . . He also chronicles systemic injustices such as the Wall that swallows land, water, and hope. Any human who reads this account and is not furious enough to be spurred into action should check his or her pulse.

—Pamela Olson, author
Fast Times in Palestine

In the summer of 2014 Richard Hardigan volunteered with the International Solidarity Movement in Palestine. *The Other Side of the Wall* reveals his personal awakening to the realities of the apartheid wall, the deadly struggles in Palestinian villages, and the violence of Israeli forces and right wing settlers. Set against the backdrop of mounting pressures culminating in the devastating seven-week assault on Gaza, Hardigan's voice moves from innocence to a deep-seated rage as he bears witness to the brutality of Israeli policies, politicians, and soldiers. In the tradition of Rachel Corrie, this book joins a growing collection of voices calling out grief and loss—making it more difficult for anyone to say, "I didn't know."

—Alice Rothchild, author
Condition Critical: Life and Death in Israel/Palestine

Cover: Palestinians standing in line at the Qalandiya checkpoint. July, 2013.
Photo by Richard Hardigan.

The Other Side of the Wall

An Eyewitness Account of the Occupation in Palestine

Richard Hardigan

Cune

The Other Side of the Wall:
An Eyewitness Account of the Occupation in Palestine
by Richard Hardigan
© 2018 Richard Hardigan
Cune Press, Seattle 2018
First Edition

Hardback	ISBN 9781614572022	$34.95
Paperback	ISBN 9781614572039	$19.95
eBook	ISBN 9781614572053	$9.99
Kindle	ISBN 9781614572046	$9.99

Library of Congress Cataloging-in-Publication Data

Names: Hardigan, Richard, author.
Title: The other side of the wall : an eyewitness account of the occupation in Palestine / by
Richard Hardigan.
Description: Seattle : Cune Press, 2018
Identifiers: LCCN 2017004385| ISBN 9781614572022 (hardback) | ISBN 9781614572039
(pbk.)
Subjects: LCSH: Arab-Israeli conflict--1993---Peace. | Peace movements--Palestine. | Pales-
tine--Politics and government--21st century.| West Bank--Politics and government--21st
century. | International Solidarity Movement.
Classification: LCC DS119.76 .H3723 2017 | DDC 320.95694--dc23
LC record available at https://lccn.loc.gov/2017004385

For the endnotes please see http://richardhardigan.com/osw/endnotes/
Photo Credits: Richard Hardigan

Bridge Between the Cultures (a series from Cune Press)

Apartheid is a Crime	Mats Svensson
Searching Jenin	Ramzy Baroud
East of the Grand Umayyad	Sami Moubayed
The Plain of Dead Cities	Bruce McLaren
Steel & Silk	Sami Moubayed
Syria – A Decade of Lost Chances	Carsten Wieland
The Road from Damascus	Scott C. Davis
A Pen of Damascus Steel	Ali Ferzat
Turning Fear into Power	Linda Sartor

 Cune   Cune Press: www.cunepress.com | www.cunepress.net

Contents

Photos

Foreword

E<small>VERY YEAR HUNDREDS OF</small> W<small>ESTERN ACTIVISTS</small> make their way to Palestine in a show of solidarity with the Palestinian people. Their intent is to provide actual help on the ground to those who are under direct and indirect occupation in the West Bank, those who are besieged in the Gaza ghetto, or those who are subject to a regime of Apartheid and discrimination inside Israel. Richard Hardigan is one of these activists.

In recent years these visitors have been seen by official Israel as constituting an existential threat. What the authorities fear in reality is not entirely clear. One can think of the wish of the government and security services to hide the oppressive reality on the ground as one major motivation. But in the age of the internet, and the relative ease with which the foreign press can still travel from Jerusalem to anywhere in the occupied territories, is there still a serious attempt to block information?

Another more sinister possibility is that what Israel wants is to maintain a fine balance between oppression and resistance, which can be easily disrupted by the activists' work both inside and outside Palestine. Life under occupation and oppression must be bearable enough so as not encourage another intifada, but ruthless enough for people to lose hope in their ability to change the reality, and perhaps even leave as a result, if they can afford it. The activist presence on the ground is the principal connection between the Palestinians and the humanity outside the borders of the Jewish state, the world that understands the reality of the occupation and oppression and wishes to show solidarity with those living under the impossible reality Israel has imposed on them for the last fifty years. So preventing such a human contact is part of a wish for consolidating control over the lives of the people who have been under occupation in a way that ensures their silence and maybe even encourages their transfer and expulsion.

This is why it is so important to continue the effort of visiting and reporting back to others what the reality on the ground is like and how best the people under occupation can be helped. The main body that visits and volunteers is the International Solidarity Movement (ISM), which Richard, the author of this book, has joined. Together with the pressure from the outside, mainly through the BDS (boycott, divestment and sanctions) campaign, this kind of activism is what the international community can offer best for the cause of peace and justice in Israel and Palestine.

Without such an effort the only remaining engagement in the West with the reality in occupied Palestine would be through the political elites and the governments of the day. However, they are not likely to change the course of action which they have adopted since the collapse of the Oslo accord. They have knowingly chosen indifference and inaction in the face of the continued criminal policies on the ground. The mainstream media and academia in the West follow suit. So it is only the active sections of the civil society who are engaged in BDS on the one hand, and the solidarity on the ground with the Palestinians on the other, that leave hope for a just and significant Western position toward peace and justice in the torn land of Palestine.

It is not only the occupied West Bank, or the besieged Gaza, that needs such solidarity and activism. The refugee camps in Lebanon, the ethnically cleansed Bedouins inside Israel and other Palestinians groups must be linked to this active solidarity as well.

***

This book is one individual story of such activism. The personal tale provides practical advice to others regarding what such activism entails. More importantly, this book presents a concise analysis of the issues at the heart of the Palestine problem. Activism of this kind requires both a clear understanding of what to face in Ben-Gurion airport, the Allenby Bridge or the Rafah crossing into Gaza, as well the possibilities of being active in the demonstrations and protests that take place daily in the West Bank.

As the book clearly shows, such activism demands a good knowledge of the history of the region and an open-minded analysis of the events of today and what people are fighting for in the future. This book has managed to do it all in one place and will be essential for both readers who are contemplating for the first time such activism and for those already deeply involved in it. Such activism, as this book illustrates so well, is more than anything else a refusal to remain silent in the face of the inhumanity and oppression which is now entering its second century.

—Ilan Pappé
Professor of History and Director of the
European Centre for Palestine Studies,
University of Exeter.

Introduction

This book is neither balanced nor neutral. I do not believe this to be a flaw. When one observes a strong man beating a helpless child or an overwhelming military force crushing a defenseless civilian population, balance is not a virtue in a point of view. The only relevant aspect of these situations is that the strong are dominating the weak. I have taken that position in this book. Neutrality is not an option. Desmond Tutu once said that "if you are neutral in situations of injustice, you have chosen the side of the oppressor. If an elephant has its foot on the tail of a mouse, and you say that you are neutral, the mouse will not appreciate your neutrality."

In the Israeli-Palestinian conflict, Israel is the elephant and the Palestinians are the mouse. It has been that way since before 1948, when the Zionists expelled three quarters of a million Palestinians from the land of Palestine to create room for a Jewish homeland, and it is still that way now. Supported almost unconditionally by its superpower patron, the United States, Israel has maintained a brutal military occupation over the West Bank and Gaza since 1967. The state of Israel now comprises seventy-nine percent of Historic Palestine, and if you include Area C in the West Bank, where the illegal settlements are located, Israel has complete control of roughly ninety-one percent of Palestine.[1] The remaining territory is administered by the Palestinian Authority, which by many Palestinians is seen as a collaborationist entity.

Many of the people that I met in the West Bank—both Palestinian and international—believe that the primary purpose of the Israeli government's harsh policies vis-à-vis the Palestinians is to make their lives as miserable as possible, thereby encouraging them to leave, whereupon it can exert even greater authority over the land. Palestinians in the West Bank face—on a regular basis—violence meted out by both soldiers and settlers, long waits at checkpoints, travel restrictions, home demolitions, theft of natural resources, unfair economic practices, arbitrary detention and arrest, long prison sentences, and countless other forms of humiliation.

The conditions in Gaza are even worse. While Israel pulled out of Gaza in 2005, it maintains de facto control over the Strip, as it enforces an inhuman and illegal blockade that keeps the population in a constant state of abject poverty. When there is resistance to Israel's policies, it punishes not just the offenders but all residents by subjecting them to massive aerial and sometimes ground campaigns that result in enormous human cost and suffering.

***

I have spent almost my entire career as a professor in the United States, but in the spring of 2008 I spent a sabbatical teaching at a university in Cairo. From 2010-2012 I took a two-year hiatus from my work in the US and accepted a position at another university in Egypt. I fell in love with the country and its warm and welcoming people, and I still count many Egyptians among my close friends. I returned to my university position in the US for the academic year 2012-2013. When the summer of 2013 arrived, however, I was back in the region, this time to improve my Arabic language skills. I enrolled in classes at Birzeit University near Ramallah in Palestine. I had previously visited Jerusalem, but this was my first extended stay in the West Bank. I had read extensively about the conflict, but it was another thing altogether to see it with my own eyes. I was shocked by the injustice that I witnessed. I visited the divided city of Hebron, where a few hundred settlers—and the 3,000 soldiers assigned to protect them—conspire to make life miserable for the local population. I traveled up to Qalqilya, a city that is almost completely surrounded by the Apartheid Wall and has consequently seen its economy devastated. I saw in Bethlehem, a tourist destination famous for its Christian sites but also a victim of the Occupation, the Wall decorated with beautiful graffiti cutting through its heart. I stood in line for hours in the sweltering heat in a long, narrow metal cage at the Qalandiya checkpoint, waiting to have an Israeli soldier issue judgment on me, deciding whether I would be allowed to pass or not.

Despite the poverty, unemployment, misery, and dejection, I found that the people maintained the Palestinian tradition of warmth and hospitality towards strangers and travelers. I also found hope. And I found resistance. I attended demonstrations in the villages of Nabi Saleh and Bil'in, where the locals were protesting against the Occupation.

By the end of the summer, I knew I had not learned as much as I wanted to about Palestine. My weekdays had been taken up with my Arabic studies, and only on weekends had I had the opportunity to travel and see what I could of the country. It had not been enough, and I knew I had to return.

Back in the US I saw an announcement for the meeting of an international but Palestinian-led organization: the International Solidarity Movement (ISM). As its name suggests, ISM is devoted to standing in solidarity with the Palestinian in their struggle against the Occupation. I had heard of ISM because of the connection with Rachel Corrie, the twenty-three-year-old activist who was killed in Gaza in 2003 while working for the organization. I had also run into a few of their members at the demonstration in Nabi Saleh, but beyond that I knew little. At that meeting, and at a few subsequent ones, I learned about some of the work that ISMers performed in Palestine. A quote in the Israeli daily newspaper *Ha'aretz* about the group, which I found in a book by scholar Norman Finkelstein,[2] made a particularly strong impression on me:

> The ISM is an international pacifist movement that draws its inspiration from a quote by Albert Einstein. "The world is a dangerous place to live; not because of the people who are evil, but because of the people who don't do anything about it."
>
> Since the start of the intifada, hundreds of the[se] foreigners, mostly students, have taken a rigorous course in nonviolent theory and practice and then been placed in Palestinian towns and villages, where they report on events at checkpoints, villages under curfew and house demolitions, help move humanitarian aid into besieged areas, and accompany ailing Palestinians to hospitals.[3]

I decided to join them in Palestine for the summer of 2014. This book is about my experiences during that time.

RAMALLAH

1
Tuesday, June 17
Arrival in Palestine

I TOOK MY XANAX PRECISELY ONE HOUR before the plane was scheduled to land at Ben Gurion International Airport in Tel Aviv. I tend to sweat when I get nervous, and I was afraid I would be nervous in about sixty minutes. I had been to Israel twice before, and only once had there been a problem at the border.

This time I was going to Palestine to work with the International Solidarity Movement, or ISM, as it is better known. As described on its website, ISM "is a Palestinian-led movement committed to resisting the long-entrenched and systematic oppression and dispossession of the Palestinian population, using non-violent, direct-action methods and principles."[1] Despite ISM's commitment to non-violence, the organization is extremely unpopular with the Israeli government. The Israeli Prime Minister's Office issued a report in 2003 that accused ISM of aiding Palestinian terrorists. The report stated that "ISM members take an active part in illegal and violent actions against IDF soldiers. At times, their activity in Judea, Samaria and the Gaza Strip is under the auspices of Palestinian terrorist organizations."[2] It is hard to take such rhetoric seriously, as the Israeli government also singles out well respected human rights organizations such as Amnesty International and Human Rights Watch for harsh criticism.

All of my interaction thus far with ISM had been very much "cloak-and-dagger." I had created a false identity and contacted the international coordinator of ISM through a phone number I obtained on its website. The conversation was short, as if it was obvious that somebody was listening, and very little information was shared. I was to call him once I arrived in Ramallah. I was told there would be two days of training, and beyond that I did not know much.

The attitude of the Israeli security services vis-à-vis ISM confuses me. It would be a simple matter for them to arrest all ISMers and deport them immediately. They bother to label ISMers as terrorists, but they do not do anything about them. I often wonder why not.

The Israeli Security Agency confirmed what I already knew about entering Israel. "Foreign left wing activists, especially ISM members, who seek entry into Israel, often do so under false pretenses, via cover stories—entry for matrimonial, tourist, religious, and other purposes—which they coordinate prior to arriving in Israel."[3] It certainly seemed that being honest at the airport about my connection to ISM would not be an option.

***

The first time I entered Israel was in 2008, when I was living in Egypt. I had traveled by bus from Cairo to Jerusalem, and I was exhausted from the ten-hour ride across the Sinai to the Red Sea town of Taba, but I was ready to face any border official the Israeli state could throw at me. As I left Egyptian soil and prepared to enter Israel, I fingered my Irish passport in my pocket. Having been born in the US to Irish parents, I am lucky to have two nationalities. I had only recently obtained my Irish papers, and I have used my American identification almost exclusively my entire life. This time, however, I decided to show the Irish passport. I was warned that an Israeli stamp would create serious problems for me in future travels to Arab countries, and I determined that the best way to avoid the stamp in my passport was to show a passport I never use. There was a second reason I was hesitant to use my American passport. It contained numerous stamps, many of which were from countries not exactly popular with the Israeli government, Iran and Syria among them.

There was no line at the passport control counter, and the young woman smiled at me.

"Citizenship?"

"Ireland." That felt strange. I had never told anybody I was Irish before. I already felt like I was lying.

"Passport, please." She took my crisp Irish passport and leafed through the pages. "Where is your Egyptian stamp?"

And that was how my first attempt at deceiving the Israeli border control system was foiled. I explained sheepishly that I had two passports, and that I just happened to have picked the Irish one to show her. She seemed unperturbed, probably because many Israelis also have two citizenships, one from the country in which they were born and grew up, and one they received from the Israeli state because their mother was Jewish.

"Where are you going?"

"Jerusalem." I had been advised to keep my answers short, to volunteer as little information as possible.

"Do you have a guide?"

"No."

"Do you have a guidebook?" I handed her the well-worn copy of the Middle East Lonely Planet my sister had lent me for the trip, and I watched her leaf through it with interest. Unfortunately, my sister has a habit of making notes in the margins of the book next to places she has either visited or intends to visit.

"So you've been to Iran?"

"Yes." The officer immediately picked up the phone, and two of her colleagues arrived to escort me to a small room with a metal desk and a few chairs. I was directed to sit down, as they conferred amongst themselves. After half an hour the questioning began. They laughed when I told them I went to Iran for vacation.

"Why would anybody want to go to Iran?"

"It's a beautiful country."

The questions continued for the next two hours, as they asked me about my grandfather's middle name, my profession, my favorite football team, etc. Sometimes they would ask the same question twice, an hour apart, to ensure that my answers did not change. It was by now quite late in the evening, and they did not seem particularly interested in my answers. Eventually they let me go.

My next crossing into the state of Israel, which took place in the summer of 2013, was more fraught with worry but ended up being much smoother. I had signed up for an Arabic class at Birzeit University in the West Bank, and the secretary of the university's Palestine and Arabic Studies program warned me that I would have to lie about my summer plans if I expected to get past Israeli security. The Israeli government does not like it if you say anything about the West Bank, and they will often turn you away and put you on the next plane out of the country if they find out you have any plans to visit it. Leo, one of my classmates in an Arabic class in the US, had relayed to me his story that he and his friend had been banned from Israel for ten years after border officials discovered that they had been lying about their intentions to enter the West Bank. (The sole exception to this rule seems to be the town of Bethlehem, and a journey to its Christian sights is considered by the Israeli government to be a legitimate activity.) On this occasion I felt relatively safe in using my Irish passport because I was flying directly from Europe, and the lack of stamps would not arouse suspicion. After telling the customs official that I wanted to visit Jerusalem, Tel Aviv, and Haifa, I managed to enter Israel for the second time.

Now I was still worried, however. Would the Israelis be suspicious if I returned a mere ten months after I left? Would they ask me about every place I visited in the past? One of the major difficulties with only pretending to be a tourist is that you do not actually do any of the things that tourists do. I tried to rectify this by reading in my Lonely Planet (just Israel this time), and I tried to memorize some popular tourist destinations, but I knew that I would not survive serious questioning.

In July of 2013, the previous year, I had had a small run-in with an official at the Qalandiya checkpoint. This checkpoint, which lies next to the refugee camp of the same name, is located approximately halfway between Ramallah and Jerusalem. It serves as the main crossing point for Palestinians who live in the northern half of the West Bank and have permission to enter Jerusalem.

In Qalandiya the Israelis have done their best to let the Palestinians know who has the power in their relationship. There are long, thin metal cages in which Palestinians have to wait their turn to be questioned by Israeli officials before they are (possibly) allowed to pass. I only went through this process once, but once was enough. I had to wait several hours in one of these cages before I finally had the chance to talk to a border guard, who seemed to treat me with as much disdain as she could muster. I was frustrated by the long wait, the heat, and the thought that the people waiting with me had to go through this procedure every day. When I was faced by a blond, pony-tailed, twenty-year-old woman sipping a Coke and joking with her friends as she determined the fate of these people passing before her, I simply lost my temper and snapped at her when she asked the usual questions.

"What were you doing in Ramallah?"

"I'm taking Arabic."

"Veeeery interesting."

Her tone and her stare left little doubt about the fact that she probably thought I should be considered highly suspicious. Eventually she allowed me to pass but not before recording my (American) passport information and making notes in her computer, possibly to scare me more than anything else.

It is this experience that was on my mind as the plane began its descent. Did the Israeli government know that I was in the West Bank? Could they tell that the Irish me was the same person as the American me? If I admitted that I had been to Ramallah, they probably would not let me in. If I lied and they caught me, they would not let me in. I decided that the best option was to deny any knowledge of the West Bank and hope for the best.

My preparation for the border crossing had been painstaking and meticulous. I cleaned my email account and removed any emails containing the words *Ramallah, Palestine, West Bank, boycott, apartheid*, and *return*. I unsub-scribed from all the activist email groups of which I was a member. I removed all the pictures from my last trip to Palestine. I figured out how to change the titles of some of the books with a Palestinian slant on my Kindle. *Life and Loathing in Greater Israel* by Max Blumenthal morphed into Leon Uris' *Exodus*, and Ilan Pappé's *The Ethnic Cleansing of Palestine* evolved into *The Human Stain* by Philip Roth. I erased *Tears of Gaza* and *Jenin Jenin* from my smartphone's list of movies I had been meaning to see. I changed the names of my Ramallah contacts on my cell phone. I changed my Facebook name. I did all of this, but I was sure there was something I had forgotten.

Luckily, the Xanax had by now taken full effect, and these questions slowly disappeared from my mind.

This time my encounter with the border official was anti-climactic. I mentioned the name, address, and telephone number of a Jewish friend I planned to visit, and I was allowed to pass. There were no questions about the previous year. Even after passing through customs, I glanced behind me nervously, in disbelief I had made it through. I did not exhale until I was sitting in the shuttle to Jerusalem, happily wedged between two ultra-or-thodox Jewish men dressed in black from head to toe.

***

After a ninety-minute shuttle ride, I arrived in Jerusalem to meet my friend Barry, with whom I was to stay the night before moving on to Ramallah the next day. We walked to the famous Education Bookshop in East Jerusalem, close to the Old City, where the owner greeted Barry warmly. The shop has hundreds and possibly thousands of titles about the Arab-Israeli conflict, and I wished I had more time to spend here. I also rued the fact that I was unable to buy any of the first-rate books, because of the problems they would almost certainly cause for me when I left Israel at the end of the summer. At best they would be seized at the airport, and at worst they would arouse so much suspicion that I would be subjected to an intense search, which could eventually lead to my deportation and banishment. Like with most first-time visitors to Israel from the US, it had taken me some time to become accustomed to the idea that a Western democracy, as Israel likes to present itself, punishes even visitors for the political views they might hold. By now however, it no longer surprised me when I heard from my German friend that his camera was seized in Berlin by El Al officials for no discernible reason, other than that he was a young university student and thus fell into the activist demographic. (It happily turned out later that the airline returned his camera to him after he landed in Berlin following his trip.)

In the bookshop I was excited to have the chance to use my Arabic for the first time since landing, but—as usual in Palestine—I was the subject of some good-natured ridicule because of my use of the Egyptian dialect, acquired during my years in Cairo. Because of Egypt's dominance of the Arab film industry, its dialect is familiar—but recognizably different—to most Palestinians, and they enjoyed giving me a hard time about it. They would practice pronouncing the hard *g* and use Egyptian forms of address, such as *Ezzayyak?* (How are you?) and *Ya basha* (Hey sir) with me. One friend describes the Egyptian dialect as "the most ghetto of all the Arabics," so I would fantasize that this lent me some extra credibility. In any case I found it flattering that they considered me as more than merely an ordinary Westerner.

We ordered *yansoon* tea and sat down at a table in a small area above the bookshop. I had first met Barry when he was a student at my university in the US, but we became close because we also took Arabic together. Only one of Barry's parents is Jewish, but he definitely identifies with the Jewish half of his ancestry. He had arrived in Israel several months earlier with a vague notion of helping to foster peace between Israelis and Palestinians. He had landed what he thought was his dream job with a pro-Palestinian non-governmental organization (NGO) in Ramallah, but a personality conflict with his boss had eventually caused him to quit. Back home his frequent visits to my office hours often morphed into discussions about the Palestinian-Israeli conflict. I told him about my experiences traveling throughout Palestine the previous summer and the many injustices that I had witnessed, and I could tell that he had trouble reconciling what he was hearing from me with what he had been told growing up. He had been raised on the standard Israeli narrative of the country's birth, but he had also seen the horrific images of the massacres during Operations Cast Lead and Pillar of Defense on television. (Operation Protective Edge was still weeks away at this time.) I was curious what effect, if any, the last six months in Israel had had on his mindset. I did not have to wait very long to find out.

In recent days the headlines in Israel had been dominated by the apparent kidnapping of three teenaged settlers just outside the West Bank settlement of Gush Etzion, near the city of Hebron. In reaction to these kidnappings, the Israeli army launched Operation Brother's Keeper, an orgy of collective punishment on the population of the West Bank, which resulted in several Palestinian deaths, hundreds of arrests, and the theft and/or destruction of millions of dollars of cash, property, and valuables. All across the West Bank there were demonstrations in response. Barry, however, was unsympathetic to their cause.

"Those Palestinians really embrace their victimhood, don't they?" he said.

Barry's answer was disheartening but not unexpected. There is not much doubt that the attitudes of many Israeli Jews towards Arabs—even Arab citizens of Israel—are quite racist, and I was guessing this had had an effect on him. That Palestinians play a lesser role in the country is reflected in the very definition of Israel as embodied in many national institutions and documents: a home for the Jews and also a Jewish and democratic state. The Israeli national anthem refers to Judaism and even Zionism. It describes the "yearning of the Jewish soul." The so-called Law of Return, passed by the Knesset in 1950, states that "every Jew has the right to come to this country as an *oleh* (immigrant)." The fact that an American Jew from Brooklyn has more of a right to live in Jerusalem than does a Palestinian who was born in East Jerusalem cannot be seen in terms that are anything but racist.

An analysis by *Ynet News* of a 2007 report by the Association for Civil Rights in Israel revealed several disturbing trends regarding the views of Israelis vis-à-vis Arabs. "Over two-thirds of Israeli teens believe Arabs to be less intelligent, uncultured, and violent. Over a third of Israeli teens fear Arabs all together."[4] The report went on to cite a poll in which fifty percent of Israeli participants said "they would not live in the same building as Arabs, would not befriend Arabs, or let their children befriend Arabs and would not let Arabs into their homes."[5]

In recent years the attitudes of Israelis regarding the Palestinians seem not to have changed much. A poll taken in 2014 by the Palestinian Center for Policy and Survey Research showed that sixty-two percent of Israelis fear being hurt by an Arab at some point in their lives.[6] A Pew poll conducted in 2016 revealed that forty-eight percent of Jewish Israelis agreed with the statement "Arabs should be expelled or transferred from Israel."[7]

These racist views are prevalent in Israeli society, and they are also reflected in some of the laws that govern the country. For example, in 2009 the Israeli Knesset passed the *Nakba* (catastrophe) Law, making it illegal to commemorate the forced expulsion by Zionists of hundreds of thousands of Palestinians from their lands between 1947 and 1949. *Nakba* Day is celebrated on May 15, which also marks Israel's day of independence. The *Nakba* is one of the most important national symbols and points of identification for Palestinians, and the *Nakba* Law is an attempt to marginalize them. In the original version of the law, a person celebrating the *Nakba* could be arrested but—buckling to international pressure—the Israelis modified the law to deny public funding to any organization that commemorated it.[8] In 2011 the Knesset passed the "Law to Revoke Citizenship for Acts Defined as Espionage and Terrorism," which, as argued by the Israeli NGO Adalah, "targets Arab citizens of Israel and makes their citizenship conditional."[9] The Admissions Committees Law of 2011 allows communities whose Jewish residents form a majority to retain their demographic composition. It gives them the opportunity to reject a request by any Israeli citizen to live in the community based on whether he is considered by a committee to be "unsuitable to the social life of the community . . . or the social and cultural fabric of the town."[10] In practice this is used as a tool to, once again, marginalize the Arabs.

According to Adalah there are currently over fifty laws "that directly or indirectly discriminate against Palestinian citizens of Israel in all areas of life, including their rights to political participation, access to land, education, state budget resources, and criminal procedures. Some of the laws also violate the rights of Palestinians living in the [Occupied Territories] and Palestinian refugees."[11]

***

After meeting with Barry I decided to go on to Ramallah that evening rather than spend the night in Jerusalem. I boarded the #18 bus from the station in East Jerusalem, and after a thirty-minute ride I arrived near al-Manara, Ramallah's central square. Although it was close to midnight, the city was noisy and alive. The streets were packed with cars, and the sidewalks were difficult to navigate with my bags. I walked down Rukab Street, one of Ramallah's busiest shopping areas, past shawarma shops, *qahwas* (local cafés), ice cream shops, and clothing stores.

Due to its proximity to Jerusalem and its location in the center of the West Bank, Ramallah has become Palestine's administrative hub. Most NGO's who work in Palestine have their headquarters here, and you can see Westerners rushing about on the streets of Ramallah and lounging in its cafés. This is not an altogether welcome phenomenon, since the Western presence has caused the cost of living to skyrocket here. The relationship between Palestinians and Western donor agencies is complicated, and the attitudes of locals towards them range from deep appreciation to extreme frustration. In particular, as journalist Ben Ehrenreich points out, the aid organizations work at the behest of their sponsors, who are allies of Israel, often to the detriment of the Pales-

"Gas the Arabs" spray painted by settlers in Hebron.

tinians.[12] However, this does not affect the centuries-old Palestinian tradition of welcoming travelers, and I felt warm as I lugged my gear down the street.

I was to meet Bill, a Canadian ISMer, at a gas station, and he was to take me to the ISM apartment, where I was to spend the next two days training and preparing for my stay in Palestine.

The apartment was located in the basement of an apartment building situated off a small dark street. Cynthia, the media coordinator, welcomed me and showed me the men's bedroom, which was packed full of mattresses and blankets. A British woman of twenty-five, Cynthia seemed to be perpetually stressed, and I believe her method of dealing with this was to never be without a lit cigarette in her mouth. Bill was the only other man staying there tonight, and he liked to sleep in the living room, so I had my choice of mattresses and blankets. I was exhausted from traveling all day, and I tried to ignore the smell as I sank into the least stained mattress I was able to find. After a short time, I fell asleep.

2
Wednesday, June 18
De-Arresting in Ramallah

Selim was the only other person who was scheduled to be trained with me, and he greeted me warmly after we had been introduced in the morning. I could tell immediately from his open manner that he and I would get along. Selim worked for a South Korean NGO that monitors human rights violations, and he wanted to volunteer with ISM for two weeks to report on the situation in Palestine. His English was poor, and despite having taken Arabic for over two years in Jordan, he was unable to speak more than a few Arabic words. I wondered how he was going to communicate with the people here in Palestine.

Selim was not Selim's real name. He had chosen an Arab name as his pseudonym, and it created confusion whenever he was introduced to Palestinians. ISMers are encouraged to use fake names for security reasons, although not everybody does. Most volunteers use a name that has some meaning to them, such as that of a grandmother or a long lost pet. Others use a variant of their real name. Miguel, for example, might choose Michael. Still others use their real name without telling anyone. I chose James, because it was the name of one my best friends in elementary school. I found it more than a little strange that I would spend several weeks living with some of these people, seeing them on a daily basis and sometimes even needing to trust them in a dangerous situation, when I did not even know their real names.

Selim and I, like everybody who volunteers with ISM, were asked to write our real names—along with our contact information—on a piece of paper, which was then placed in a sealed envelope. Our ISM names were written on the envelope, which would be opened only if we were arrested or killed and our families needed to be contacted. If nothing serious occurred at the end of our time in Palestine, the information would be destroyed.

I believe that the main purpose of ISM's two-day training program is to frighten you. The living room of the apartment in Ramallah is adorned with posters of martyrs of the Palestinian cause including ISMers. Stacey, a long-time member of ISM, once told me that the only famous ISMers are the dead ones, but she did not like to talk about them herself.

Among them is Rachel Corrie, a twenty-three-year-old American woman, who was killed in March of 2003 while she was attempting to block an Israeli Defense Forces (IDF) armored bulldozer from demolishing the home of a Palestinian pharmacist in Gaza. Both Rachel's image and her story are well known throughout the West Bank, and there is even a Rachel Corrie restaurant near the Baab a-Zawiya checkpoint in Hebron. (A year later, I was surprised to see a mural of Rachel's face on a building in the Palestinian refugee camp of Shatila in Beirut. When I asked a friend in Lebanon about it, he told me that every Palestinian knows Rachel Corrie. There is now even a street in Tehran named after her.[1])

Rachel's death is still a source of controversy. ISM witnesses said that the bulldozer deliberately ran her over, while the army placed the blame squarely on her shoulders, going so far—in a report summarizing the results of its subsequent investigation of the events—as to claim that she was not run over by a bulldozer at all, but that she was killed by a slab of concrete.[2][3][4] The army also claimed that it was not in the process of demolishing the home at the time, although it did destroy it later. In 2005 Human Rights Watch issued a report that heavily criticized the army's investigation, stating that "the impartiality and professionalism of the Israeli investigation into Corrie's death are highly questionable."[5] Rachel's parents filed a civil lawsuit against the state of Israel, but this was dismissed in 2012.[6] They subsequently filed an appeal of this verdict, asking for a single US dollar as compensation for her death. They charged that she had been killed intentionally or that at minimum the soldiers had acted with reckless abandon. The appeal was rejected in 2015.[7]

I could not imagine the pain that Rachel's tragic death must have caused her parents. For the past eleven years they had been fighting court battles and watching the Israeli army attempt to brand their daughter a terrorist in order to avoid having to claim responsibility. How could they possibly deal with this for so long and keep fighting for justice for her? It made me think of my own mother.

In the month following Rachel Corrie's death, the IDF shot two ISM activists. The twenty-four-year-old American Brian Avery was shot in the face and sustained permanent injuries, while the twenty-one-year-old Briton Thomas Hurndall received a bullet to the back of the skull as he was escorting Palestinian children to safety in Gaza. Hurndall fell into a coma and died a few months later. The same month, Israeli Army Chief of Staff Moshe Ya'alon, who later served as Minister of Defense, ordered his forces "to take the ISM out,"[8] and in the next few weeks activists were rounded up, and the ISM office in Beit Sahour was raided.[9] According to an ISM spokesperson, however, the authorities had been exerting pressure on foreign activists all along. Between April and August of 2002, for example, the Israeli government deported roughly fifty ISMers.[10]

Ayman was the international coordinator for ISM, and part of his job was to prepare us to deal with the various types of Israeli armed forces. There are four types of forces—the regular police, the border police, the riot police and the regular army—and we were told how to recognize each of them by their uniforms. We could be facing elements of all four of these organizations, and it was important to understand their differences in terms of the techniques and weapons they utilize and the rights they have. The police forces tend to be made up of professionals. These are individuals who have chosen a line of work that brings them into conflict situations, and they tend to be violent. Many of them are from the margins of Israeli society, and they feel that committing increased violence against the Palestinians will enable them to prove their loyalty to the state. In other words, these are the ones to be the wariest of. Regular IDF soldiers, on the other hand, are more likely to be less enthusiastic, since they are forced by the draft to wear the uniform. These are mostly average eighteen-to-twenty-year-olds from all walks of life. We heard stories that sometimes IDF soldiers even shoot to miss during demonstrations in the West Bank.

One of the most frightening lessons we were taught involved de-arresting. De-arresting refers to rescuing others from being arrested, and the techniques we were told about are apparently remarkably effective. The idea behind de-arresting somebody is that it is much more difficult for a soldier to arrest or detain two people than it is to arrest or detain one, and this increased level of difficulty is supposed to decrease the soldiers' motivation to continue what they have started. If one individual is in the midst of being detained, another is to lock arms with the first one, thus making their arrest take longer. This delay allows a third person to join the fray and lock arms with the first two. Eventually enough people are wrapped up together to persuade the soldiers that it is simply not worth the effort to complete the arrest. The prospect of getting involved in a physical altercation with soldiers and grappling with them seemed terrifying to me, but Ayman told us that it was something we had to do when the opportunity arose, that there was no choice.

"When a Palestinian is arrested, he is usually sent to prison for at least a month, where he can be subjected to harsh conditions and even torture. Internationals, on the other hand, will at worst be deported and banned from entering Israel. Israeli activists who are arrested have the easiest time, as they are released after a day at the most," he said.

Ayman also indicated that we should not fear being shot by Israeli soldiers at close quarters. The last thing they wanted to do was shoot an international activist, so even if a soldier ordered me to put up my hands or get on the ground, I was simply to ignore him. However, I decided that if an Israeli soldier pointed a gun at my head and insisted that I kneel on the ground in front of him, I would do exactly that. The posters of the dead ISMers on the walls of the living room convinced me that this course of action was the safest one.

Every Friday there are demonstrations all over the West Bank. Some of them are about specific grievances in the locale of the demonstration, such as the closure of a road, while others are against the Occupation in general. Still others, occurring less regularly, are organized to show resistance to particular events, such as the massacres in Gaza. One of the most famous of the weekly demonstrations occurs in the village of Bil'in, which has been depicted in the award winning documentary *Five Broken Cameras*. (ISM actually donated the second of these five cameras to director Iyad Burnat.)

The dictionary defines solidarity as "union or fellowship arising from common responsibilities and interests." One of ISM's main tenets is that of standing in solidarity with the Palestinians who are resisting the Occupation. One of the ways in which we achieve this is by attending one of the demonstrations every Friday. This serves several purposes, some of which are practical, while others have greater symbolic and emotional value. The Israeli occupation of the West Bank began in 1967 and, despite all of the UN resolutions and the peace processes, little progress has been made towards ending it. In fact, the lives of Palestinians have been progressively getting worse as Israel strengthens its stranglehold on every aspect of Palestinian life. Many Palestinians get the sense that their struggle for freedom has been forgotten by the rest of the world, and that they have been left to fend for themselves against a regional military superpower that is bent on their destruction. It therefore means a great deal to local activists and ordinary people alike, when they see internationals participate in the demonstrations. They understand that internationals have traveled from far and wide to partake in their struggle, and it heartens them. They read the Western—and especially the American—media's mostly one-sided take on the conflict, and they see the American opinion polls indicating overwhelming public support for Israel's position. But our presence shows them that there are people out there who know and who care.

A more practical effect of ISM's presence at the demonstrations is that Israeli forces are less likely to commit violent acts in the presence of internationals. Israel is extremely conscious about its image, and IDF soldiers are much more careful with their weapons when they know Westerners are watching, especially when their cameras are turned on. A nightmare scenario for the IDF would be the killing of an international activist, as we saw in the fallout of the Rachel Corrie case. Even the killing of unarmed Palestinians on camera can be bad publicity for the army. I was told on several occasions that Palestinian activists tend to take advantage of the Israeli reluctance to fire on internationals by placing them in more dangerous situations, using them as human shields, but I never had that experience myself.

3
Thursday, June 19
Nablus or Hebron?

ISM had teams in Ramallah, Nablus, Hebron, and Gaza, although the Gaza team was essentially its own entity, a situation enforced by the isolation of the Gaza Strip. The Ramallah team consisted mostly of part-timers and administrators, and it was recommended that Selim and I choose to join the teams in Nablus or Hebron. We were supposed to decide at the end of the second day of training, but we had not yet made up our minds. The very last session was about regional updates. These were presentations given by the regional coordinators of the Nablus and Hebron teams.

After lunch on Thursday, Ayman talked about what was probably the most concrete symbol of the Israeli occupation of Palestine: the Apartheid Wall.

Also called a separation barrier or security fence, the Apartheid Wall, of which approximately eighty percent has been completed, runs roughly along the Green Line, the border that divides Israel from the West Bank and East Jerusalem. Ostensibly the purpose of the Wall is to give Israel a measure of protection against the suicide bombers that enter Israel from the West Bank. Construction of it began on April 14, 2002, during the Second Intifada, when Palestinian suicide attacks inside Israel were occurring frequently. That year fifty-five Palestinian suicide bombings were carried out from the West Bank. In the following years, the numbers began to decrease. In 2003, there were twenty-five such attacks, fourteen in 2004, seven in 2005, four in 2006, and one in 2007. The statistics seem to indicate that the Wall to a large extent achieved its purpose but, as journalist Ben White wrote in 2014, the data are quite misleading.[1]

The international community, via the judicial branch of the UN, the International Court of Justice (ICJ), has made its views on the Wall clear. On July 9, 2004, it stated that it considered the Wall to be contrary to international law. Regarding the issue of the purpose of the Wall as a weapon against terrorism, the court argued that Israel naturally has the right to maintain its security, but that "it is not convinced that the specific course Israel has chosen for the wall was necessary to attain its security objectives and . . . finds that the construction of the wall constitutes breaches by Israel of various of its obligations under the applicable international humanitarian law and human rights instruments."[2]

If the primary reason for the construction of the Wall was indeed to prevent suicide bombers from entering Israel, then the additional beneficial consequences for Israel and the deleterious effects on Palestinian society are mere coincidence. Though the Wall was intended to run along the Green Line, roughly eighty-five percent of it actually runs east of it, thus annexing large tracts of Palestinian land to the Israeli state. As the court states, "Israel states that the placement of the Wall inside the West Bank in some places is due to topographical considerations, as tall buildings or hills on the Palestinian side would negate the Wall's effectiveness as a weapon against terrorism."[3] In such cases, the ICJ explains, Israel was required to build the Wall inside Israel proper. According to data issued by the United Nations Office for the Coordination of Humanitarian Affairs (OCHA), approximately ten percent of the area of the West Bank will lie to the west of the Wall, along with some 30,000 Palestinians.[4] This area includes a large percentage of settlers living in the West Bank. The placement of the Wall thus creates changes in Palestine that Israel will claim constitute "facts on the ground" that are not subject to negotiation in any future settlement with the Palestinians.

***

The regional coordinator for Nablus was a twenty-two-year-old Spaniard named Charlie, whose shorn head made him look even younger. Charlie had been with ISM for three months, and he spoke with a confidence that comes with experience. He told us that at his very first demonstration in Palestine, in the nearby village of Ni'lin, eight people were shot with live ammunition. Quite an introduction to life with ISM. He also informed us of the projects that the Nablus team had been engaged in for the last several months, although at the moment he was by himself in Nablus. He said he hoped Selim and I would join him.

The main difference between the situation in Nablus and the one in Hebron was that there were no settlements in the city of Nablus. This also implied that although the Israeli army did come into Nablus—and especially its refugee camps—on a regular basis, there was no permanent military presence in the city itself. Most of the problems occurred in the surrounding villages, which were targets of both the settlers living nearby and the army. Because these villages were relatively spread out, ISMers had to do a great deal of traveling, usually in the ubiquitous *services* (pronounced serveeces), yellow vans that carry passengers along routes that snake all over the West Bank. A consequence of this distance was that the activists usually arrived at a

Small boy and his bicycle by the Apartheid Wall in Bethlehem.

problem-spot hours after the army or the settlers had left, and they ended up merely taking pictures and interviewing the victims. The overall impression that Charlie gave me was that there was not much confrontation with soldiers or settlers, a fact that gave me comfort. Charlie himself seemed knowledgeable, organized, competent and, most importantly, trustworthy.

The contrast with Olaf, the coordinator for Hebron, could not have been starker. Although I would end up working with him for a week in Nablus and become deeply appreciative of his qualities, his first impression was not positive and, after the first few minutes of his presentation, I decided I would go to Nablus. Olaf was a twenty-two-year-old Danish activist. He was disheveled, heavily tattooed, and it was clear that he had not taken a shower in at least a week. He had scribbled a few notes on a napkin, which he struggled to decipher as he explained to us what was happening in Hebron.

Hebron was the only city in the West Bank in which the settlers actually lived inside the city, next to—and often literally on top of—their Palestinian neighbors. There were a few hundred settlers living in Hebron and roughly 3,000 soldiers assigned to protect them. The situation was volatile, and there was a great deal of conflict between the Palestinians and the settlers, and between the Palestinians and the army, and ISMers tried to navigate between the combatants. Olaf told us that even though soldiers could often be very cruel to the Palestinians and sometimes shot and even killed them, they did have to follow orders, and that this somehow limited the damage they could do. Settlers, on the other hand, were only limited by their conscience and therefore much more dangerous.

In general, one found economic settlers and ideological settlers in the West Bank. Economic settlers ended up living in the settlements because of the financial incentives offered by the Israeli government, and they tended to be much less fanatical than the ideological settlers, who believed they were doing God's work. In Hebron the large majority of settlers were of the latter variety and posed a much greater threat to the Palestinians and to the ISMers who stood in solidarity with them. Many of them carried IDF-issued M-16's over their shoulder and seemed to wander H2—the Israeli-controlled neighborhood of Hebron—looking for trouble. I recalled from my visit to Hebron the previous summer that, after I lost my way in Tel Rumeida in H2, a small Palestinian boy indicated a route to me that was safe "because there are no settlers there, only soldiers."

***

As Selim and I lingered over our dinner of beef kebabs at the shop a short walk down the street, we talked not about Nablus but about Ni'lin. Friday was demonstration day, and Selim and I had decided to go to Ni'lin while a few other ISMers would go to Nabi Saleh. All the talk of soldiers, bullets, and teargas during the training sessions had frightened me and, although I was anxious to start moving beyond training, my feelings about this protest were mixed. Foremost in my mind were the recent shootings during a demonstration in the West Bank town of Beitunia, close to Israel's notorious Ofer prison. The protest took place on May 15, *Nakba* Day, a commemoration of the *Nakba* of 1948, when hundreds of thousands of Palestinians fled or were expelled from their homes by Zionist forces. During the demonstration Israeli soldiers shot and killed two Palestinian youths, an event that happened to have been captured on camera. Most disturbing was that neither one of the boys was doing anything of consequence just before being shot. (Witnesses did say that both boys had been throwing rocks at soldiers earlier.) For me it was difficult to imagine a soldier firing on and killing boys that posed no threat to him or her. The video had a chilling effect on me. One second a boy was just walking towards his friends, and the next second he was on the ground, mortally wounded. The boy's fellow protesters carried him to an ambulance, but he later died. It made me consider my own situation.

If a soldier was going to shoot an unarmed boy, what would stop him from shooting me? I assumed he had been told not to shoot foreigners, especially light-skinned ones, but still, this was a soldier who hated what I was doing here, and he knew he was not subject to severe punishment no matter what he did. Why would he not just shoot me?

Israeli officials indicated that the soldier had been suspended for "firing his weapon without authorization," but they also said that the army had been using only plastic-coated bullets on that day. Witnesses at the scene explained that plastic-coated bullets had been used in addition to live ammunition. Doctors who examined the bodies stated that both boys had been killed by bullets that exited their bodies after passing through their chests. This indicated that live ammunition must have been used, since plastic-coated bullets do not even break the skin unless fired from very close range. This was certainly neither the first nor the last time that the Israeli army lied, and in fact I would be exposed to its lies on a more personal level several times during my stay.

Israeli soldiers in Palestinian neighborhood in Hebron.

4
Friday, June 20
Teargas in Ni'lin

ON FRIDAY MORNING AT TEN O'CLOCK, Olaf, Selim, Jason (a twenty-seven-year-old British law student), and I left the ISM apartment and walked in silence to the *service* station just north of Rukab Street, from which we would take a short *service* ride to Ni'lin.

I like to wear shorts and sandals even when the weather is cool, but on this occasion we were all wearing long pants and running shoes. The long pants were out of respect for the locals in the village, who tended to be more conservative than the residents in big cities such as Ramallah, but also to protect ourselves from the various weapons we expected the Israeli soldiers to use against us. We wore running shoes in case the demonstration turned dangerous, and we had to make a run for it.

We also all had with us a *keffiyeh*, the traditional Arab headdress originally worn as protection from sunburn, dust, and sand, but which in recent decades had become a symbol of the Palestinian resistance. For us the *keffiyehs* had a dual purpose, as they were supposed to provide a measure of protection against teargas on the one hand, while we also used them to hide our faces. Olaf carried with him a gas mask, which would serve both purposes better than a *keffiyeh*.

In one of the protests that I had attended in Bil'in the previous year, I had noticed an Israeli soldier standing behind a camera with a long telephoto lens mounted on a tripod. When I asked a friend about this, I was told that the soldiers took photos of all activists at demonstrations and sent the pictures to a central database that could be accessed by officials at border crossings. These could then be used to deny entry, since it was illegal for anybody to attend protests in the West Bank. I did not know if it was just a rumor intended to frighten us, but I never heard of an activist being detained at the border because of a picture taken at a demonstration. For Palestinians on the other hand the threat was real, and I knew of several who were arrested simply because of a photo that proved their presence at a protest.

There was one weapon used by the Israelis for which you could not prepare, and it is one feared by every Palestinian. At some demonstrations you could see what looked like a water truck, with a cannon mounted on its roof. "The cannon," said Mariam Barghouti, a Ramallah-based activist and writer, "projects water at a high velocity so there is a risk of that injuring you."[1] However, the fear it inspired in Palestinians and activists was derived not from the velocity of the liquid but rather its contents. For the water used was not ordinary water. Instead the truck fired what is known as skunk water, an incredibly foul smelling substance. It is said that skunk water is so malodorous, that if unlucky enough to be struck by it, one can detect its presence on clothes up to five years later.

"Due to its intense smell that gnaws at your nostrils, it makes it difficult to breathe," Barghouti told *The Electronic Intifada*. "If you only get sprayed with it, that is an agony you have to live with for a few days to a few weeks. The water lingers on your skin to a point when you want to rip your skin off."[2]

A Palestinian friend once told me that his people would do anything to save an international activist at a demonstration: anything, that is, except face the dreaded skunk water.

We passed by what we called the Nutella store, a shop dedicated solely to the sale of Nutella products. The previous summer this store had been an object of ridicule for some of the international students at Birzeit, but on this day my mind was on something else. Jason and Olaf were both experienced activists and did not appear nervous, while I felt apprehensive and assumed Selim had similar feelings. Selim was the only one among us who had a family, including a three-year-old daughter, so I could imagine that his fears were of a different sort altogether. I had been to three demonstrations in the previous year—one at Nabi Saleh and two at Bil'in—and I had met ISMers at all of them, but this was to be my first demo as a member of ISM.

Ni'lin is a village of 5,000 inhabitants that lies approximately twenty kilometers to the northwest of Ramallah. It is situated roughly three kilometers from the Green Line, along which part of the Apartheid Wall was constructed. To build this section of the Wall, the Israeli army confiscated one-third of Ni'lin's territory.

Land has been stolen from the village of Ni'lin for a long time. Before the *Nakba* of 1948, Ni'lin was made up of 58,000 *dunams* of land (a *dunam* is roughly 900 square meters), of which 40,000 were annexed to the Israeli state after the conclusion of the war.[3] After the Six-Day War of 1967, several Israeli settlements, as well as roads to service them, were built on village land, taking away an additional 8,000 *dunams*.[4] Much of the land taken by the Israelis was of high agricultural quality, and hundreds of olive trees were also lost.

As is so often the case in this part of the world, the scarcity of water resources plays an enormous role in local politics. The private Israeli company Mekerot has controlled the water since 1967.[5] According to the Ni'lin media group, "settlers living in the surrounding settlements can access four times more water than Palestinians, and pay five times less for it than the Palestinian owners of the water sources."[6] In addition, during the hot summer months Israel will deny Palestinians access to their own water, thus forcing them to purchase additional water tanks at hugely inflated prices.[7]

The confiscation of so much of Ni'lin's agricultural land forced many villagers to perform menial labor in Israel. In a cruel twist of fate, the construction of the Wall made it much more difficult for most people to travel to Israel for this purpose. Furthermore, Israel cancelled large numbers of work permits for the villagers. As a result, Israel's policies have been responsible for a disastrous increase in unemployment and consequently poverty in Ni'lin. The Ni'lin media group estimates that the unemployment rate in the village hovers at approximately sixty percent.[8]

In July of 2008 the villagers began to fight back. There were almost daily demonstrations against the barrier, and the army retaliated by cruelly clamping down on the village. It imposed a curfew, and soldiers fired teargas, rubber-coated steel bullets, and even live ammunition. On July 9, three villagers were hit with live fire.[9] The images of rock-throwing youngsters defending their land by facing off against heavily armed soldiers who were surrounding bulldozers captured the attention of many Westerners, and international activists began to join the demonstrations.

In the same month of July, 2008, the Israeli human rights organization B'Tselem published a video taken by a teenaged Palestinian girl during a protest at Ni'lin. The video contained footage of a Palestinian, who was being detained, standing next to an Israeli officer. Another soldier, who was standing a few feet in front of the handcuffed and blindfolded Palestinian, suddenly shot a rubber-coated steel bullet into his leg. After an investigation, both soldiers were charged with improper conduct, but after human rights organizations protested against the leniency of the charges, the charges were augmented. Eventually both soldiers were convicted, the officer with attempted threats and the other soldier with unlawful use of a weapon. The former was given a suspended sentence with deferred promotion for two years, while the latter, who was a sergeant, was demoted to private.[10]

In that case the victim was "only" shot in the leg, but later that same month an eleven-year-old child was shot in the forehead with live ammunition and killed during clashes with Israeli soldiers in Ni'lin.[11] One day later another teen was shot in the head with a rubber-coated steel bullet. He was pronounced dead on August 4.[12] During a demonstration in Ni'lin against Israel's assault on Gaza in December of 2008, two more young men were shot and killed.[13] In June of 2009, yet another victim lost his life in Ni'lin.[14]

The deaths of so many—and the injuries of scores more—during demonstrations at Ni'lin were frightening, but I told myself that this protest was going to be similar to the ones I had attended the previous year in Bil'in and Nabi Saleh. My very first one had taken place at Nabi Saleh, and after the initial shock of realizing that soldiers were actually trying to hurt me, and after running away from the teargas canisters hurtling through the air in my direction, I had felt reasonably safe. I knew, or at least hoped, that once I reached the protest area, my memories of those demonstrations would come back, and I would feel better.

After a half-hour *service* ride from Ramallah, we were dropped off in Ni'lin, where we were supposed to meet our village contact. At each demonstration site—Ni'lin, Bil'in, Nabi Saleh, and Kufr Qaddum—ISM has local contacts who help facilitate our participation in the demonstration and connect us with leaders of the protest.

The weather was hot and dry, and the sun was blinding. The streets were deserted—as is most often the case on Fridays—except for a forlorn dog who was picking through a pile of garbage in the hopes of finding a morsel of food.

Our contact at Ni'lin was Fahmi, a thirty-year-old member of the Palestinian Red Crescent Society, and we were supposed to meet him at the Red Crescent apartment just off the main square. Fahmi was not there when we arrived, but he had left us a key, and we thankfully entered the air-conditioned apartment to rest before the demonstration. I noticed some holes in the wall of a room facing the square, and Olaf, who had been there several times before, explained to me that they had been caused by Israeli army fire a few years earlier. I was not sure whether the holes had been left there out of neglect or as a reminder that life in the West Bank was dangerous. I decided that it was neglect, since there were plenty of other indicators of the dangers of life in Palestine.

Members of ISM are supposed to stay in pairs at demonstrations, and both members of a pair are required to watch out for each other. Even though Jason and Olaf were much more experienced than Selim and me, they decided to pair up, since they both wanted to be close to the action, while Selim and I preferred to hang back, where we thought it would be safer. Olaf always took his expensive camera with him to the demos, and he liked to be at the front in order to capture as much of the action as possible. I thought Jason was just crazy, and the next few weeks only confirmed that my first impressions of him were correct.

I was worried about being paired with Selim not only because he was inexperienced, but also because I was concerned about communicating with him. Many of my conversations with him during the last few days had ended in complete confusion, because he simply had not understood me. Even worse, he would often pretend to comprehend what I was saying when in reality he had no clue. I pictured this becoming a serious issue if the protest turned violent and good communication became paramount.

All of the weekly protests in the West Bank begin shortly after the midday prayer in the early afternoon, the hottest time of the day. Fahmi and Alim, his colleague with the Red Crescent Society, returned to the apartment to pick us up and take us to the site of the protest in their red and white ambulance. Their role was to wait at the demonstration and treat the injured at the scene if the wounds were not severe or take the victims to a nearby hospital if necessary. I had a great deal of admiration for these men, as they were risking their lives for their people in exchange for very little pay.

After a five-minute drive through the town and then along a dirt road, we were let off near a small grove of trees, where we sat in the shade and waited. Next to us were six boys who appeared to be between ten and twelve years old. Some were sitting on the ground, leaning against a tree trunk and swatting at flies that were buzzing around them, while others had set up a Coke bottle a few yards away and were trying to hit it with small stones.

The demonstrations at Ni'lin are attended by international activists on a semi-regular basis, and the boys did not seem particularly interested in us. They did perk up a bit when I chatted with them in Arabic, as most foreign visitors know not much more than a few phrases in the local language. Scattered all around us were small groups of men, both young and old. I guessed there were approximately one hundred of us, and everybody appeared to be waiting.

After a few minutes we heard the *imam's* sermon emanate from a loudspeaker that had been set up nearby. The sermon lasted about thirty minutes, and then the people in the grove began to pray. I had attended prayer at mosques in Egypt, and I had always found the experience soothing. Muslim prayer is very communal, and it leaves me with a warm feeling when I am lucky enough to experience it. The men line up in rows and perform their prostrations, bowing together, so close to each other that they are almost touching. If a worshiper shows up late, instead of finding a comfortable spot for himself, he will start his prayer next to the man at the end of the last row. Islam is a very egalitarian religion, and you see doctors and lawyers pray next to farmers and old men next to children.

The prayer ended, and I took a deep breath, as I knew that the action was about to begin.

I could not see the Apartheid Wall from the grove of trees, but I knew that the road we began walking along led right to it. As planned Selim and I were near the end of the procession of fifty or so men and children that seemed to be heading in the direction of the Wall, while Jason and Olaf were somewhere near the middle. The procession was being led by a middle-aged man who was carrying a Palestinian flag and shouting into a bullhorn.

"Soldiers, why are you here? These are our homes. Why don't you go back to your families, so that we can go back to ours? You have taken almost all of our land!"

The man's words were angry, but his voice sounded resigned and tired, as if he had lost all hope. But here he was, leading his village in this protest against the armed forces occupying the land of his people.

We turned a corner, and all of a sudden we saw them. There were about twenty of them, clustered in small groups of four or five. Each group was on a hill overlooking the area to our left. The soldiers were dressed in green, and they were all wearing helmets and carrying rifles.

They were about 300 meters away, and at that distance I could not imagine them being a threat to us. I felt somehow relieved that they appeared so small, not even really human.

As the procession continued along the road, the soldiers suddenly began firing teargas in our direction. I wondered why they were doing this. As far as I could tell, nobody had thrown a stone or made a threatening gesture of any kind. We were merely shouting and walking towards the Wall. As the streaks of teargas filled the sky, some of the protesters remained on the road, while others, including Selim and me, scampered into the bushes nearby.

Although it happens occasionally, it is relatively unusual to be hit directly by a teargas canister, and the main concern is not to inhale the gas. This requires determining the direction of the wind and then reacting accordingly. It is important not to run, since running uses up much more oxygen than walking. Of course this is much easier said than done, since the natural reaction when enveloped in a cloud of teargas is simply to run in the opposite direction from which the teargas is fired. In addition, the wind changes direction frequently, so it is often difficult to decide where safety is.

On this occasion I managed to inhale only a little of the teargas. It is a sensation that I remembered perfectly from the previous summer and that could best be described as severe burning of the lungs and eyes. About half an hour later, the skin burns where it has come into contact with the gas.

As I contemplated the effects of teargas, I heard the scream of "Bullets! They're shooting!" It turned out later that these were plastic-coated steel bullets, which I thought at the time were unlikely to cause serious harm unless fired from very close range. It was still unnerving to know that there were projectiles flying through the air in my direction, and I fell to the ground.

"Everything ok, James?" I could not tell whether Olaf was seriously concerned, or whether he was making fun of me, but he was grinning.

"Look what I found!" He was proudly holding a black rubber bullet that he claimed had missed him by a few feet. He said he had heard it whirring as it passed by him. I felt more than a little ashamed. My twenty-two-year-old colleague laughed at a rubber bullet that had barely missed his head as he continued to take photos, while I, on the other hand, fell to the ground at the first sign of danger. I rose and headed back towards the road.

"Watch out! Watch out! It's coming at your head!" The warning came from a middle-aged man wearing an Orlando Magic jersey whose English was nearly accent-free. He grabbed me and pulled me to the side, as I watched a teargas canister land harmlessly ten meters behind where I had been standing.

Israeli army regulations, as well as international law, require that teargas not be fired directly at protesters. Instead the canisters must be fired at an angle of forty-five degrees above the horizontal. This rule is generally ignored by Israeli soldiers, and there are cases of protesters being injured or even killed by teargas canisters fired directly at them. A famous example is that of Bassem Abu Rahmeh, whose death in the nearby village of Bil'in was documented in the film *Five Broken Cameras*. Bassem, affectionately known by the local children as *pheel* (elephant), was shot in the chest by a teargas canister during a protest and later died.

"You have to be more careful," the man with the Magic basketball jersey said to me. "These soldiers aren't kidding around." I thanked him and looked around for Jason, Olaf or Selim, but none of them could be found. They had probably scattered to escape the latest teargas barrage. I was now back on the road and could see that the soldiers were still on the hills and pointing their rifles at the protesters, but at this point much of the teargas had dissipated, and it seemed that the soldiers had lost interest in the demonstration.

As I watched the soldiers on the hill I hoped that the demo was mostly over, since I was getting tired of the stress of being fired upon. My throat hurt and my eyes were tearing. Suddenly, I noticed a metallic object hurtling end over end and flying towards me. I could see teargas emanating from one of its ends, forming white billowing clouds that formed beautiful images against the backdrop of the deep blue sky. As it was flying towards me, I had to squint to avoid the sunlight that was reflecting from it. I watched the canister follow its parabolic arc and land a few feet in front of me, and I saw mounds of earth being displaced by the impact. The clumps of earth scattered in all directions, but they were not enough to slow the inertia of the canister. After it hit the ground, it slowly but inexorably continued on its path. I knew I should move to get out of the way, but I was too slow. The canister seemed to be moving in slow motion, but I was even slower. And then suddenly it passed over my head and was gone. And I was still standing in the same spot, alive and unhurt.

I realized that what I had done had been incredibly stupid. It had seemed to me that the demonstration was winding down. I had relaxed for one second, an act that almost had disastrous consequences for me. It dawned on me that this was a serious and extremely dangerous business. These soldiers were adamant about inflicting harm on the people they saw as their enemies. I vowed never to let my guard down again.

Although I was fine, the situation reminded me of the case of Tristan Anderson, about which I had read just a few days earlier. On March 13, 2009, at a protest in the same village of Ni'lin, the thirty-seven-year-old Anderson, an American activist volunteering with ISM, was shot in the right corner of his forehead with a high velocity teargas canister fired by Israeli border police. The bullet "broke his skull, penetrated his right eye and devastated his frontal lobe."[15] After being treated in a Tel Aviv hospital for fifteen months, Anderson returned to the US, but he is still struggling with the injuries he sustained on that day in Ni'lin. In chronic pain, he is blind in his right eye, and he is paralyzed on the left and dominant side of his body.

After the demonstration Olaf, Jason, Selim, and I waited at the side of the road near the grove of trees. According to them, five protesters had been hurt, and all injuries, mostly from the inhalation of teargas, had been minor. After a few minutes, Fahmi and Alim picked us up in their ambulance and drove us back to their office in the center of Ni'lin.

All of the demonstrations I had attended in Palestine the previous summer had been followed by sumptuous feasts, and this one was no different. The two Red Crescent medics prepared a huge traditional meal of beef and rice for themselves and us, a total of six people. I felt guilty that these men were now in the kitchen cooking for us. They were the ones living in poverty and under occupation, and they had just come from a highly stressful situation in which they were treating wounded protesters while being shot at with rubber bullets and high velocity teargas canisters. We were just visitors, spending a few months of our summer vacations witnessing their suffering, after which we would return to our normal lives back home. But I had long ago given up protesting against the hospitality of the Palestinians, and I dug in gratefully, secure in the knowledge that I was safe for at least another day.

NABLUS

5
Saturday, June 21
Our Home in Nablus

SELIM AND I TOOK THE ONE-AND-A-HALF-HOUR *service* ride from Ramallah to Nablus. Although the distance from Ramallah to Nablus is only thirty-six kilometers, the road conditions, the circuitousness of the route, and multiple checkpoints conspire to make the journey last at least ninety minutes and sometimes much longer. The road passes by the infamous Ofer prison, where two Palestinian youths were shot and killed during a demonstration several weeks earlier, an incident that was captured on video.

Ofer prison has a reputation that extends throughout the West Bank. It holds roughly 1,000 Palestinian prisoners, including children, who are housed in terrible conditions and reportedly regularly subjected to torture. Some of the prisoners have been charged and convicted, while others are simply under administrative detention.

Administrative detention allows the Israeli government to hold Palestinian prisoners without charge for up to six months. According to B'Tselem, there are currently close to 500 Palestinians in prison under this measure, and thousands have suffered this fate over the years. B'Tselem states that "due to the substantial injury to due process inherent in this measure, international law stipulates that it may be exercised only in very exceptional cases – and then only as a last possible resort, when there are no other means available to prevent the danger. Nevertheless, Israeli authorities routinely employ administrative detention."[1]

Ofer prison is well known also because of the high number of children incarcerated there. In 2010 *Ha'aretz* reported on Israel's dismal record when it comes to protecting children, especially in the Occupied Territories. The article also comments on the distinction between Israel's definition of a child in Israel proper versus in the West Bank.

"Military orders applying to the occupied territories define a child as under the age of sixteen, although Israeli civilian law defines a child as under eighteen, the committee found. The UN Convention on the Rights of the Child also defines a child as under eighteen."

The Israeli human rights group Machsome Watch Organization regularly monitors military courts, and two of its observers wrote a report on their visit to the court in Ofer in 2010. That day twenty-four children stood trial, most of whom appeared to be fifteen or sixteen years old. Typical was the case of Allam Yusuf Bader Za'ekik, aged fifteen, who was charged with "hurling objects at people or property." Allam, whose father is disabled, had been on his way home from work after an altercation with his boss, who had refused to pay him. As he was walking, settlers passed by and pelted him with rocks, and because of Allam's foul mood, he had retaliated. Allam's father had not worked in the last eleven years, and Allam had been working weekends to help pay his older sister's university tuition. His lawyer asked the judge to take Allam's family's economic situation into account. The judge responded by sentencing Allam to four months in jail and giving him an additional suspended sentence of six months, but she did make an exception by not fining him.[2]

The road snaked past the prison and through the hills, which were dotted with settlements. We passed several checkpoints, none of which were manned, and we finally entered Nablus.

Charlie, who was both the financial coordinator for ISM and the regional coordinator for the Nablus team, picked us up from the *service* station and showed us to the apartment. He had been alone in the Nablus apartment for several days, and he seemed happy to see our somewhat familiar faces.

The downtown area of Nablus was packed with street vendors, who were selling everything from fruits and vegetables to t-shirts and vacuum cleaners. The air was filled with shouts as women holding crying children in their arms jostled with old men on the narrow sidewalks. As we passed through the main square, also known as the *Duwar*, the smell of kebabs being grilled made my mouth water. We walked by a falafel shop that Charlie told us was the best place in town for that. You could buy two falafel balls for three shekels and then stuff as many onions, green peppers and assorted other vegetables into a pita pocket as you could fit. Next door a group of three fully-veiled women dressed in black were rifling through a bin in a clothing store that featured mannequins wearing lingerie. Then there was a small shop selling freshly squeezed lemon and orange juices.

After a twenty-minute walk we finally turned one last corner and entered a small alley along which our apartment was located. Two small black kittens eyed us suspiciously as we passed the garbage dumpster they were sitting on. The front door of the two-story building was narrow, and I could barely squeeze through with my backpack. Climbing the even narrower stairs, I passed by the apartment of our downstairs neighbors, separated from the staircase only by a sheet, and I could hear a television set playing at high volume behind it.

The minute I entered the apartment, I knew it belonged to ISM. There were posters, some of which were the same as the ones in the Ramallah apartment. Most featured pictures of various victims of the Occupation, both ISMers and Palestinians with no connection to ISM. Another showed the brother of one of our contacts who had been in prison for the last three years. Others were more general. Among them was a very poignant poster, entitled *El Awda* (the return), that showed animated characters struggling to return to their homes. One of the figures was lying on the ground, having been shot, while another was dragging his body forward, wearing a chain with a key around his neck. It reminded me of a story related to me by my Arabic professor at Birzeit University the previous summer. He told me about his ninety-eight-year-old grandmother, who was evicted from her home during the *Nakba* of 1948 and who still carried the key to her house around her neck, hoping that she would one day be allowed to return.

There were three bedrooms in the apartment, two large ones for men and women, respectively, and another smaller one that could be used by anybody. Men and women are not allowed to sleep in the same room in any ISM apartment. Since there are usually more men than women at any time, women enjoy more comfortable sleeping arrangements, although to call them comfortable at all would be a big stretch to a middle-class Westerner. There are no beds, only mattresses and blankets. Each room holds as many as five people at a time, and there were occasions later in the summer where even that number was exceeded. In early July, there were thirteen of us in the house, and bedrooms were not the biggest problem. That honor fell to the bathroom. There was only one in the Nablus apartment, which often caused us a great deal of frustration.

6
Sunday, June 22
Four Bullets and a Funeral

Hadi was a journalist who occasionally gave ISM information about breaking news. He told Charlie that a man had been murdered by Israeli soldiers in al-Ain refugee camp the night before. He was going to a local hospital to get more information, and we could join him if we wanted to. Charlie, Selim and I walked to the *Duwar*, where we hopped in a taxi.

After a ten-minute ride we arrived at the hospital, where dozens of young men seemed to be waiting. Charlie introduced us to Hadi, a well-dressed man who appeared to be in his late twenties. He pointed out an old bent man who he said was the victim's father. The man was receiving what I assumed to be consolatory hugs and kisses from some of the others waiting nearby.

Plastered on one of the hospital doors was a poster of the victim. I could read his name, Ahmed Saeed Saud Khaled. Next to Ahmed's face was an image of a young Yasser Arafat, and below were pictures of the Golden Dome of the Rock and Al-Aqsa mosque in Jerusalem. The Palestinian flag was flying above the entire scene. I could not make out the whole sentence directly below the flag, but I did manage to pick out the word *shaheed*, which means martyr in Arabic. It was a poster typical of the victims of the Occupation, which you could see all over the West Bank, especially in Nablus, which has a long history of resistance to the Occupation.

A man in his late thirties saw me examining the poster and approached me, introducing himself as Marwan. After the usual pleasantries, he told me that he had graduated from an-Najah University, reportedly the best university in all of Palestine, but that he could not find work because of the economic devastation caused by the Israeli occupation. He showed me his deformed hands, which he told me had been broken by Israeli soldiers during the First Intifada, and he said his injuries prevented him from performing any manual tasks. I knew about then Prime Minister Yitzhak Rabin's famous instructions for soldiers to break the bones of the Palestinians,[1] but this was the first time I had seen the results of this policy in person.

Charlie had a meeting with another contact, and he took Selim with him, saying he would be back in a couple of hours and that I should try to find out exactly what happened in al-Ain camp the night before.

Marwan pointed towards a group of young men, smoking in the shade of a tree at the edge of the hospital parking lot.

"That's his brother," he said. "You should ask him what happened."

Most people in Nablus, and especially those living in the refugee camps, speak either little or no English. I approached the dozen or so men, most of whom were in their twenties, and went up to a man who, dressed in black, was leaning against a car. He made room for me against the car, and he shook my hand.

"I'm sorry for the martyr. May God bless him," I said in Arabic. The second sentence is often said to the family or friends of anybody who dies, while the first is for victims of the Occupation. The man's name was Imran, and he asked me if I was a journalist. (Since there are almost no tourists in Nablus, internationals generally fall into one of two categories: NGO workers or journalists.) The ISM training had frightened me enough not to tell anyone that I worked for that organization, a practice that I abandoned a few weeks later.

"I am a journalist, and I believe that the only way to end the Occupation is for Israel's main benefactor to stop enabling Israel. The only way that is going to happen is if enough people in the United States put pressure on the government to stop funding Israel. And the best way to bring that about is to ensure that the American public is aware of what's going on here. Americans are not bad people. If they knew about the suffering of the Palestinians and the brutality of the Israeli regime, they would be outraged. But they just don't know. Most newspapers and television news programs don't provide that kind of information. That is what my job is," I answered.

I was not sure that I believed my own little speech, especially that the main reason for the American public's apathy regarding the conflict was simply ignorance. Throughout my time in Palestine, I would post links to articles about some of the more egregious acts of Israeli violence on Facebook, but not much attention was paid to them. It was extremely frustrating to see that people appeared to care more about what they had for lunch than about the suffering of innocents a world away. I told myself it was something about social media that I did not understand. Perhaps most people turned to social media as a way to escape from everyday life, not to be faced with a reality of suffering and injustice.

In a voice that seemed to get angrier as his story continued, Imran told me how Ahmed had died. Ahmed, who was mentally handicapped, had been praying in the mosque in al-Ain camp at around midnight, and when he emerged from the entrance of the mosque, Israeli soldiers shouted at him to stop. Because of the perpetual presence of Israeli soldiers, most Palestinians know a smattering of Hebrew, especially words connected to the Occupation, such as *stop*, *arrest*, *identification*, etc. But Ahmed did not understand what the soldiers wanted from him, and he continued on his way home. The Israelis then shot him four times: once in the stomach and three times in the chest. At the time I could not figure out whether Ahmed had died immediately or in the hospital, but he did not live to see the next day. Imran's voice was shaking now.

"What did he do? Nothing! How was he a threat to the soldiers? He wasn't right in the head, and they just shot him!"

It was a story that was difficult to hear. As I now watched Ahmed's father talk to reporters in front of the main hospital doors, I tried to imagine what it must be like for the family. They lived in a refugee camp in abject poverty. The land and home of their grandparents had been stolen from them, and they were forced to live this miserable existence. Every day they were subjected to various forms of humiliation, and I could guess that their only consolation was their family. And now their son had been snatched from them for no reason at all. How was any of this ok?

And what about the soldiers? What had they been thinking? Ahmed clearly had not been a threat to them, but could they have seen things differently? They were products of the Israeli education system, and they most likely believed that Arabs were all terrorists who wanted to kill them. Probably mostly eighteen or nineteen-year-olds, they must have been nervous, surrounded by the enemy, in the middle of the night, when a young man refused an order.

So they shot him—not in the legs, as they do so often at demonstrations—but in the chest, and not once or twice, but four times. I could not accept that they had done this out of fear. This was a simple disregard for the value of a human life. I wondered whether the soldier who actually pulled the trigger had any emotional reaction. Did he feel at least a little remorseful? I would be asking myself these sorts of questions throughout the summer.

An ambulance now arrived at the hospital, purportedly carrying the body of Ahmed from an-Najah University, where an autopsy had taken place. Here the body was to be prepared for its delivery to the cemetery. As the ambulance backed up to the doors of the hospital, the crowd converged on it, hoping to get a glimpse of the body as the medics carried it the short distance from the vehicle to the doors. I could see Ahmed's father watching as he paced back and forth near a garbage dumpster, while his brother seemed to be facing in the opposite direction, doing everything in his power not to watch.

Judging from some of the conversations I had, it seemed that most of the people in the crowd were not connected to the victim or at best had known him only fleetingly. As in the rest of the West Bank, unemployment is pervasive in Nablus, and I assumed most of the young men here fell into that category. But they were Palestinians, victims of the same forces that had claimed Ahmed's life, and this sharing gave them a connection to the victim and his family and friends, a connection that I lacked.

I felt out of place here, uncomfortable because of my skin color, my height, and my clothing. I knew this feeling was my own insecurity, as most of the people here were very kind to me. Nevertheless, my feeling that I was an outsider caused me to hang back when the crowd pressed towards Ahmed's body as it was being carried into the hospital to be prepared.

After thirty minutes or so the body reemerged, wrapped in a Palestinian flag and lying on a stretcher that was being carried by six men. Ahmed's head was uncovered, with only a black and white *keffiyeh* wrapped around his forehead. As the body was carried by the bearers, it was jostled quite a bit, and the head lolled back and forth with regularity.

The last time I had seen a dead body was two years earlier in Cairo. I was on a microbus on the road from the Giza metro station to the pyramids, and all of sudden I saw a taxi stopped in the middle of the street with its windshield completely missing. Next to the car two men were carrying a blood-spattered body that was not moving. The scene was grisly, but what made it more shocking to me was the manner in which the men were carrying the body. One of them was holding the victim by the feet and the other by the hands, and they did not seem too concerned with what was happening to the rest of the body, as it was knocked here against the car and there against a street lamp. The disdain with which they were treating the body only emphasized how little life it contained, how dead it really was.

The condition of Ahmed's body differed from that of the Egyptian taxi driver because great care was taken to treat it as gently as possible. Despite those efforts, it was still jostled on the stretcher. The sight of the body added a dose of realism to the entire scene. Until that point I had just been part of a story, a character in a novel perhaps. There was no denying it now. This was real. This man was dead.

A crowd of roughly a hundred men followed the stretcher bearers as they left the hospital grounds and began to carry Ahmed's body through the streets of Nablus. The crowd by this time seemed angry. Deep and resonant chants affirmed both the greatness of God and the evil of Israel. Big yellow flags were everywhere, which indicated that the family of the victim, and probably most of the residents of al-Ain refugee camp, were supporters of Fatah, the Palestinian nationalist movement founded by the late Yasser Arafat, and which was the dominant faction in the Palestinian Authority (PA). The procession moved quickly, and Ahmed's father, an old frail man, trailed behind, fingering his prayer beads. Occasionally somebody up ahead would slow down and wait for him and then embrace him, whispering consoling words into his ear.

After thirty minutes we arrived at the entrance of the refugee camp. Among the crowd I saw Imran, who had told me the story of Ahmed's killing back at the hospital. I saw now that he had a severe limp and had probably taken a taxi back to the camp. He smiled and offered to walk with me as we followed Ahmed's body through the camp. The route from the hospital to the camp had followed along some of the wide main streets of Nablus. The roads in al-Ain camp, however, are extremely narrow, as they are in all refugee camps in the West Bank. In addition, the camp is built on the side of one of the two mountains that surround Nablus, and the procession slowed considerably as it wound its way uphill through the narrow streets.

Imran told me that the plan was to carry Ahmed's body up the hill to his house, where his mother and his female relatives were waiting to say goodbye to him. I could picture Ahmed's mother hunched over his body, kissing his forehead, knowing that she had only a few minutes before he would be taken from her again. It was a depressing image that made me want to cry.

I did not follow the body as it made its voyage up to his house, and when the body was brought back down and into a mosque for a service, I did not go inside with it. The camp cemetery was next to the mosque, and I did follow the procession to the cemetery, where I watched them lower the body into the ground. At this point, as I watched the grieving family and friends, I felt very much like an intruder, and even though Imran insisted that I stay and have coffee with him, I thanked him and decided to head back. I walked down to the entrance of the camp and hailed a taxi that took me back to the *Duwar*, from which I walked to the apartment.

***

I could see bluish smoke curling through the dining room from the kitchen. Charlie and two others were sitting on white plastic chairs and smoking, while Selim was listening to their conversation. I was introduced to Rafaela and Giuseppe, two Italian activists who were staying in the house with us.

"There are rumors that the Israeli army is going to come into Nablus tonight, and we have to decide what to do in case that happens."

Rafaela's voice had that grainy quality that can only come from a lifetime of heavy smoking. A woman who appeared to be in her late thirties, Rafaela worked for an international organization called International Women's Peace Service, more commonly referred to by its acronym, IWPS. The ranks of that organization were so depleted at that time that they had decided to close their house in the nearby village of Madama, and ISM had been gracious enough to allow her to stay in the ISM apartment in Nablus. A colleague of hers, Cathy, would be joining us in a few days.

Giuseppe, who also appeared to be in his late thirties, had arrived in Palestine only a week earlier. Unlike Rafaela, he was not a long-time activist. He had recently been fired from his work as a software engineer and decided he needed a break from his life in Italy before he reentered the job market. He told me he was planning to stay in Palestine for several months.

Neither Rafaela's nor Giuseppe's English was very good, and it was difficult to communicate with them. When they were alone together, they usually spoke Italian, a habit that on occasion they continued to follow even in the presence of their non-Italian colleagues.

***

On June 12, 2014, a week before my arrival in Palestine, three Israeli teenagers had gone missing near the West Bank city of Hebron. The teenagers were seminary students in the settlement of Gush Etzion, and according to witnesses, had last been seen trying to hitchhike home late in the evening. Israeli Prime Minister Benjamin Netanyahu immediately claimed that the boys were abducted by a terrorist organization and that he held the Fatah-controlled PA responsible.[2] He also claimed that the incident was a direct result of the attempt to create a Hamas-Fatah unity government.

Representatives of both Hamas and Fatah had met in Gaza in April, just a few months earlier, and signed an agreement designed to end the years-long rift between the two parties. An outraged Israel had let its opposition to the pact be known by bombing the Gaza Strip immediately after it was announced.[3] And now Netanyahu was placing the blame for the teenagers' disappearance on this rapprochement.

"To my regret," he said, "this event underscores what we have been saying—myself, the Defense Minister and the Government of Israel—for many months: The pact with Hamas has led to very harsh results, results which are the exact opposite of advancing peace between us and the Palestinians."[4]

The Israeli government determined almost immediately after their disappearance that the settlers had already been killed.[5] However, the authorities saw this as an opportunity not to be missed. They issued a gag order to the journalists who knew that the teens were dead and were thus able to keep the truth from the general public. On the pretext that the teens needed to be rescued, Netanyahu was able to whip the country into a frenzy, using the public's ignorance of the events to pursue his goal of disrupting the agreement between Hamas and Fatah.

The Israeli response to the kidnapping was swift and unequivocal, especially in Hebron, where the army closed all main entrances to the city and stationed soldiers everywhere. According to B'Tselem, Israeli forces prevented Palestinians with permits to work in Israel from entering the country. In addition, they forbade all Hebron males between the ages of fifteen and fifty from traveling. There were also many reports of soldiers blowing up doors of Palestinian homes and acting with extreme violence in an effort to locate the missing teenagers.[6]

This collective punishment was not limited to Hebron, as the army entered villages and towns all over the West Bank. A week after the teenagers were last seen, "over 300 Palestinians have been arrested since the operation began, among them Hamas charity workers, Hamas-affiliated journalists, and the head of the Palestinian Legislative Council, who is a member of the party.

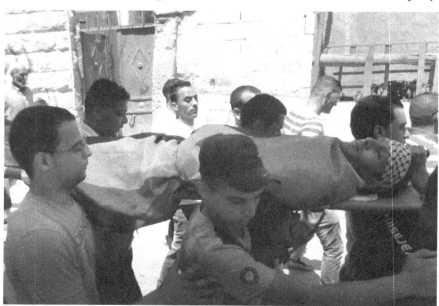

Ahmed Saeed Saud Khaled's body being carried through the streets of al-Ain refugee camp.

Hundreds of thousands of residents of Hebron remain under closure. Soldiers have raided homes and stores, and have confiscated weapons, computers, and security camera footage, leaving behind them a trail of destruction."[7]

***

Charlie told us that Nablus was not immune from the Israeli rage, and that the army had entered downtown Nablus the night before. He explained that you always had some warning before this happened.

"Before the Israeli army enters a city, it lets the PA know, so that there are no clashes between the two forces. When you see that there is no PA, you know that the Israelis are coming."

The point of the meeting in the kitchen was to decide on a course of action in case the soldiers came to Nablus again.

"There was lots of gunfire all night long, and I was scared out of my wits that the soldiers would enter the apartment," Charlie told us.

He explained that because of the rule that no ISMer was allowed to work alone, he had been forced to stay in the apartment. Now that there were five of us here, some of us would actually be able to go outside, an option that did not sound very appealing to me. However, since the role of ISM in Palestine was both to act in solidarity with the Palestinians and to record and monitor Israeli abuses, these clashes afforded us the perfect opportunity to fulfill that purpose.

It is another ISM rule that nobody is forced to engage in an action that he or she is uncomfortable with, and that there is absolutely no pressure to do so. Charlie explained that these clashes were very dangerous, and that the soldiers would probably be using live ammunition. It was a scary thought to be running around the crowded streets at night being fired at with teargas and real bullets.

We agreed that three of us could go while two stayed behind. Some of the choices were obvious. It was decided that Giuseppe, whose formal ISM training would take place the following week and who did not have even the rudimentary knowledge of Israeli weapons and techniques that the rest of us possessed, should remain behind. Rafaela, on the other hand, who had achieved a modicum of fame in Italy with a documentary she had shot and always had her video camera within reach, insisted on going out to film. She also refused to go without at least one experienced activist at her side, which meant that Charlie should accompany her, to which he agreed. Selim, whose enthusiasm on occasion seemed to exceed his prudence, also indicated that he wanted to go out to meet the Israelis in the event that there were clashes.

This meant that I would stay. I let out a deep breath that I hoped the others did not notice, but I did feel a twinge of guilt and shame. I felt like a coward.

That night the Israeli army did indeed enter Nablus, but we did not find out until the following day. The soldiers restricted themselves to terrorizing the local refugee camps and did not make an appearance in the downtown area.

***

I did not sleep well. It was the end of my first day in Nablus, and I was still grappling with my feelings about everything. Israeli soldiers had shot and killed a mentally handicapped man in cold blood, and I had witnessed his funeral and talked to his friends. I had met a man who had had his hands broken by soldiers. Meanwhile the IDF was running rampant all over the West Bank, punishing ordinary Palestinian civilians for a kidnapping that Netanyahu had accused Hamas of perpetrating. I kept wondering whether the army would come to Nablus. Would we be woken in the middle of the night and called to go outside? Even though Giuseppe and I would stay home in that case, what if the soldiers entered the apartment? I could not imagine what I would do if ten or twenty armed soldiers broke down our door and ransacked the flat. We had discussed that we would destroy all of the computers in the house, as they contained the phone numbers of all of our local contacts, information that could send them to jail for months or longer. All of this talk was nice in theory, but the possibility of these events actually occurring frightened me.

7
Monday, June 23
Abdullah

A YOUNG PALESTINIAN was sitting in front of the computer in the living room. It was the first time I had seen Abdullah, but we would become very close during the summer. Abdullah was twenty-three years old, and he was from Awerta, a village to the West of Nablus. He worked in construction, a job he despised, but at the same time he was studying English at al-Quds Open University where he was taking online courses. Abdullah was short and skinny, and I had trouble imagining him swinging a hammer or maneuvering a wheelbarrow on a construction site. He said his dream was to move to the West.

"This place is shit. Life here is shit. There is no future. America, Canada, Italy. Anywhere would be fine, but I'd love to go to Sweden," he told me. "The nicest activists come from Sweden."

Abdullah had been with ISM for the last six months. On occasion he stayed in the apartment overnight, but most of the time he would help out with ISM when he was not working and then return to Awerta to spend the night. Abdullah was invaluable to ISM in many ways, not least because of his Arabic. When local contacts, most of whom spoke limited English at best, called the coordinator phone, Charlie would invariably hand them off to Abdullah. My own Arabic was fairly limited and of the Egyptian variety, and trying to understand Palestinian Arabic on the telephone was next to impossible for me. The fact that many of our contacts came from the countryside and had thick accents made things even more problematic. None of the other international activists currently in the ISM house in Nablus spoke any Arabic at all, so without Abdullah we would have had serious communications issues.

Abdullah's contributions were not only linguistic. Having grown up nearby, he knew a great deal about the area. He knew a taxi driver that would take us to the weekly demonstrations in Kufr Qaddum without overcharging us drastically, and he knew the best place in Nablus to get kebabs. He knew from which station the *service* to Azzun left, and he knew whom to call if we wanted to visit a refugee camp. This kind of knowledge could only come from having lived in the area for years, and none of the internationals could claim to have done that.

Charlie and Abdullah appeared to be great friends. Abdullah would hug Charlie randomly, and since the latter would be leaving ISM in a matter of days, Abdullah was depressed. He said that both the best and worst parts of working with ISM were being involved with the activists. The best part was getting to know them, and the worst was having to say goodbye to them. Although there are exceptions, most ISMers stay in Palestine for less than two weeks and there is a lot of turnover.

"It's difficult to always have to say goodbye," Abdullah told me on more than one occasion.

***

In the evening things were relatively quiet in Nablus. Abdullah had gone home, Giuseppe and Rafaela were having what seemed to be an angry conversation in Italian, while Selim was talking to his wife on Viber. I had been selected as Charlie's replacement as ISM's financial coordinator, and he was explaining to me some of the duties that I would be responsible for once he left.

ISM has very few sources of income, most of which is derived from individual donations. Harvard Law Professor Alan Dershowitz,[1] quoting from a 2003 *Jerusalem Post* article,[2] states that ISM receives funding from both Hamas and the PA, a claim so absurd it made me laugh out loud when I heard it. If Dershowitz had ever set foot in any of the ISM apartments, he certainly would have realized immediately that Hamas would never bother with an organization such as ours. (Scholar Norman Finkelstein points out that the *Post*'s claim, denied by ISM, is based entirely on an anonymous "senior security government source."[3])

Finkelstein,[4] quoting from Dershowitz,[5] notes that the latter describes ISM as "a radical pro-Palestinian group of zealots . . . who are one-sided supporters of Palestinian terrorism. . . . They serve as human shields, working closely with Palestinian terrorist groups. . . . They do not support peace. Instead, these zealots advocate the victory of Palestinian terrorism over Israeli self-defense. . . . The media should stop referring to these people as peace activists and should call them what they are: active supporters and facilitators of Palestinian terrorism."

8
Tuesday, June 24
Midnight Invasion in Madama

RAFAELA, SELIM AND I made the fifteen-minute walk to the bus station on the eastern side of town. We were on our way to Madama, a village where, according to one of our contacts, the Israeli army had engaged in a violent raid the previous night.

It was very hot, and the stench of garbage assaulted my nostrils as we passed the market next to the station. Fruit and vegetable vendors were spraying water on their wares to make them look more appealing. Two cats were waiting next to the kebab stand, hoping the owner was in a generous mood and would throw them a few scraps. Mothers were carrying bags of fruit in one hand while they were leading their youngest children with the other. Selim smiled at everyone that looked at us, but Rafaela strode purposefully with her head forward.

We arrived at the station, but the *service* to Madama was empty. There were three of us, which meant that we would have to wait for four more passengers before the driver would be willing to leave. Rafaela waited inside the *service*, but Selim and I sat on the curb in the shade offered by a lonely tree. I asked if it was hard for him to be away from his wife and daughter.

"It's not too bad. I Skype or Viber them every day. The best part of my day is when I see the look on my daughter's face when she recognizes me on her computer screen."

I wondered if Selim's experience was more difficult for him because of the cultural differences between him and most of the other ISMers. He was the only Asian, and his English was too limited to have a deep conversation with anybody. Rafaela and Giuseppe were not much better at speaking English, but at least they could communicate with each other. Selim did not have anyone. Whom would he tell about his feelings when a victim of Israeli abuse recounted his experiences to him? Whom would he confide in when he felt afraid of being hurt in an upcoming demonstration? I imagined he would discuss these thoughts with his wife as I did with my family, but I often found it very helpful to talk about these issues with my colleagues, who were having feelings similar to my own and could probably understand them much better than most others.

After roughly half an hour four women dressed all in black boarded the *service*, and we were ready to leave.

"It is really hot today, isn't it?" I commented in Arabic to the woman sitting on my left. She laughed and turned to her friends, saying something that was mostly unintelligible except for the word *ajnabi*, which means foreigner, whereupon they all broke out in laughter.

I always enjoyed seeing the reaction of Palestinians when they heard me speaking Arabic. I knew there was no malice in their laughter. An Egyptian friend once told me that Arabs are very happy when they see a foreigner speaking their language. They see it as a great compliment. A stranger in Cairo once thanked me profusely for learning Arabic after I had asked him for directions. I found it very touching.

The countryside around Nablus is very hilly, and the road curved as we drove through several villages. In one village that consisted of a few stone houses, we saw four men holding down a cow, which was lying on its side as a fifth was standing next to it with a knife. The cow was writhing fiercely, and its big brown eyes seemed to be filled with desperation.

Selim told me later that he actually saw the man try to cut the cow's throat, sawing at it vigorously, but that it was not working because the knife was too dull. The situation reminded me of a recurring dream I have, in which I come across a badly injured rabbit. In the dream I know I should kill the rabbit to put it out of its misery, and I start to beat it, but it will just not die. It keeps thrashing around, doing all it can to escape, but I just keep beating it. It is a terrible dream. There is a scene in *Crime and Punishment* that I still recall twenty-five years after I read it. Raskolnikov is staying in an inn, and he encounters a man who beats his horse to death. Dostoyevsky describes the killing in great detail in a scene that goes on for several pages, and it is very difficult to read. The horse's terrible suffering goes on for what seems like hours as it gets beaten until you think it is finally dead. But then it somehow stirs, and the man starts to beat it again to the point where it does finally die. I sometimes wonder if my dreams are somehow related to that poor horse.

***

The president of the Madama Popular Committee, Latif Khawaja, welcomed us in his office. He was about thirty years old, much younger than I had expected, given his important position in the village. He did not appear to be in a good mood, and he glowered at us from behind his expansive desk.

"The army came around midnight last night. There were about fifty soldiers that came in jeeps, and they raided one hundred homes in our village. They had guns, and they were very aggressive. They took eighty men to the elementary school where they held them until five o'clock in the morning.

"Usually the soldiers come every once in a while, maybe once a week, but now because of the teenagers they come every day. They want to punish us."

"But the teenagers were kidnapped near Hebron. What does this have to do with you?" Latif chuckled, as if amused by my naiveté.

"Those boys were not kidnapped. Everybody knows that. It's just an excuse for Netanyahu to do whatever he wants. He wants to make life unbearable for Palestinians so that we will leave. But what can he do? Life has been unbearable for the last seventy years. Is he going to make it worse? We are still here, and we will never leave, no matter what they do to us." I asked him if the soldiers had arrested anybody.

"No. They kept the men in the school for five hours, but then they released them all. They blindfolded them and handcuffed them behind their backs, but then they let them go."

I wanted to make sure I had the details right. I mimicked being blindfolded, and I held my hands behind me, asking Selim to pretend to handcuff me. Latif nodded. I knew that it was against international law to blindfold prisoners. It was also stipulated that if handcuffs are used, they must be put on the prisoners' hands with their arms in front, not behind their backs. These soldiers had broken the law. But Latif was not finished.

"My brother, Fawez, was also taken to the school, but he was kept separate from the others. The soldiers beat him. Perhaps you would like to talk to him? He is busy now, but he will be here in a couple of hours."

I told Latif that I very much wanted to interview his brother, but that I still had a few questions for him. I had read of several instances of Israeli soldiers stealing merchandise and cash from some of the houses they raided, and I asked Latif if the soldiers had taken anything.

"They stole the money from Wafiq Khawaja's house. A lot. Do you want to talk to him? My assistant will take you there. By the time you get back, Fawez will be here, and you can talk to him, too."

Latif's assistant led us to the house of Wafiq Khawaja, which was a ten-minute walk up the hill. Outside we met two women in Western dress who looked they might have been in their sixties, a strange sight here in this tiny village an hour outside of Nablus. In broken English they told us they were with B'Tselem and that they were here to talk to Khawaja about the previous night. Apparently the soldiers had ransacked his house and stolen a large amount of money. They had an interpreter with them, and they invited us to take part in the interview, to which we readily agreed.

For an hour Selim and I sat in Wafiq Khawaja's living room, listening to his account of the previous night's events. We shook hands with Wafiq and two of his adult sons as they welcomed us into their living room. I was surprised to see that it was clean, given that the soldiers had been here so recently.

"All of us have been working since early morning to clean up the mess they made," said Wafiq. "They can come in here and destroy everything, but we have to make the house clean again. If we cry and feel sorry for ourselves, it means they win."

On his digital camera he showed us pictures he had taken the night before. They showed holes in the walls and upended shelves whose contents were strewn about everywhere. As I was to see throughout the summer, this was standard fare for a visit from the Israeli army. Wafiq was in his early sixties, and he had worked in Israel for several years before he finally returned home to Madama in 2000. He continued with his story.

"The soldiers knocked on the door at one o'clock. They came here, because they knew about the money. That's the first thing they said after they entered. Where is the money? When I said I didn't have any, they began to drill holes in the walls, and they threatened to destroy the entire building. They ripped open the sofas and chairs, and they tore everything off the walls."

Wafiq motioned to one of his sons, who offered to show us the kitchen, where the damage was the worst. I wanted to stay to hear the rest of the story, but Selim rose to follow the young man into the kitchen.

Wafiq paused for a few seconds as if the recalling of the story brought back the events themselves. He said he had already recounted the story to some local journalists this morning, and he said it was difficult to go through this again. His son, who himself was clearly upset, patted him on the shoulder and urged him to go on.

"These people want to help us, father. We should tell them." Wafiq took a deep breath.

"I made a lot of money in Israel, and I brought it all back with me. I don't believe in banks. They are not safe. So I kept it all in the house. And now it's gone. It was hidden underneath a cupboard and in some other places around the house. They found it and took it. It was everything we had, and we will never get it back." One of the B'Tselem women mumbled something to the translator in Hebrew.

"How much money did they steal?" the interpreter asked Wafiq. The amount was staggering: 200,000 shekels (roughly $70,000). The soldiers also made off with two laptops and several mobile phones. I wanted to ask him the same question I had asked President Khawaja. Why did he think the army came here? But I knew I would get the same answer. It was collective punishment for the kidnapping of the three teenagers.

Latif Khawaja's assistant, who had disappeared, now returned to the living room.

"Fawez is waiting for you at the office. Do you want to come to talk to him?" I thanked Wafiq for his hospitality and promised to write a report for ISM.

"The more people know about this," I told him, "the more likely it is that you will get your money back." The look on his face as I uttered these words made me realize how ridiculous my statement must have seemed to him. It was clear that he would never see a shekel of that money again.

We arrived at the office of the Madama Popular Committee, where we found Fawez Khawaja, the brother of the committee president. Fawez, a muscular twenty-two-year-old, was dressed in his blue policeman's uniform, replete with big black boots. After the customary introductions and inquiries about the health of our families, Fawez explained to us what had happened to him during the night.

"The army broke down our door at one in the morning. There were fifteen soldiers. They were very aggressive. They wanted to go into the rooms of my sisters, but I asked them to wait so the girls could get dressed. This made them angry, and the captain started to swear at me. I lost my temper. How can these people just come into my house and disrespect me and my sisters like that? I'm a policeman. They are soldiers. What is the difference? They are supposed to uphold the law."

Fawez' hands were trembling as he was recounting his story. I could not imagine the pain and humiliation he was feeling. I tried to think about what I would have done in a similar situation.

When I would go for walks with my sister in Cairo during my time there, groups of young men would on occasion harass her. They would surround her and make lewd remarks, not knowing that I spoke Arabic. This happened to her more when I was not around, but it did occur once or twice when I was with her. It made me furious, but there was nothing I could do. The one time that sticks out most in my mind, there were roughly ten of them, and to engage them would have been foolhardy. I was left feeling impotent and humiliated. I assumed that Fawez' feelings were similar, only more extreme, because he had to go through experiences like this on a regular basis.

Fawez continued his story.

"When the captain swore at me, I could not take it. I wanted to punch him, but I only swore back at him. Three or four of them then started to beat me, kicking me in my stomach and my back. This went on for several minutes. They dragged me to their jeep, where they continued to beat me. I begged them to stop, but they just ignored me. They put a blindfold over my eyes and handcuffed me behind my back. They drove me to the school, and they kept me in a room by myself. At one point they held me by the throat and drove their knees into my back. They released me at four o'clock in the morning, and I was allowed to go home."

To ensure that I understood exactly what had happened, Fawez demonstrated. He grabbed my throat, pushed my hands far behind my back and dug his knee into my lower back. It was exceedingly painful, and I yelled at him to stop. I could not imagine what it would have been like to endure this in the middle of the night with soldiers who were not play-acting.

"Why do they not respect human rights?" Fawez asked me. "I'm a policeman, and I know about human rights. Why don't they?"

***

It was a quiet ride back to Nablus for Selim and me, both us focused on our own thoughts. I had read many stories about the mistreatment of the Palestinians at the hands of the Israelis, but what those stories did not convey was how commonplace and ordinary these occurrences really were. What had happened at Madama the night before was ordinary. The army had raided a village, ransacked some houses, stolen some money, and beaten some people. This was not serious enough to merit a mention in any newspaper or in any online news outlet that I could find. I supposed it made ISM's work all the more important because without us this story never would have seen the light of day. We would write a report that would show up on ISM's webpage, and many of our followers would find out what had happened. They would be outraged, but chances were that if they were reading ISM's stories, they were already informed about what was occurring in Palestine. We needed to reach people that did not know what the Israeli army was doing. We needed ordinary people all over the world to find out, because I still believed that the world would not continue to allow this kind of injustice to continue if it only knew. Because that was always the excuse: we did not know. It is what they said after the Holocaust, and it is what they said after the genocides in Cambodia and Rwanda. We did not know.

On the way back to Nablus we passed the spot where the cow had been slaughtered earlier in the day. I looked for traces of it, but I saw none. Perhaps I was mistaken about which village it had taken place in.

9
Wednesday, June 25
Gunfire in the Streets

IN THE EVENING WE HEARD A GREAT DEAL of gunfire near the apartment. It reminded me of my experiences during the January 25 revolution in Cairo.

Living and working in Egypt at the time, I had been traveling abroad and returned on January 28 to find the country in the midst of an uprising. Living in an apartment a short subway ride from Tahrir Square, I spent most evenings that first tumultuous week listening to the gunfire outside, punctuated on occasion by frightened screams. I had no idea who was responsible for the gunfire or whether I was in danger. Was it policemen? Soldiers? Looters who had broken into the police stations after the police had abandoned them? Maybe it was the prisoners who, according to rumors, had broken out of the nearby Tora prison and were now running wild all over the city. Perhaps it was the vigilante groups organized by the local religious authorities to protect the neighborhood from the looters. I had no idea what was happening. There were only rumors, and that is what created such fear for me.

I tried to protect myself by staying away from the windows and by blocking my front door with the enormous dining room table just in case somebody got the idea to break in. I even placed money on the table as a last resort, but I definitely did not feel safe.

I ended up spending a couple of days joining the protesters at Tahrir, but I will always remember those first few days huddled in my apartment listening to the gunfire as the most frightening. After the first few days the gunfire eventually became simple background noise to me, and I ceased being so afraid.

These thoughts were swirling through my mind as I sat in the ISM apartment and listened to these sounds, which were so similar to the ones I had heard in Egypt. Again I was frightened, and again it was because I did not know what was happening.

During one particularly long round of gunfire, Charlie's phone rang. One of our contacts informed him that the army was involved in clashes in the *Duwar*, only a ten-minute walk from the apartment. He wanted us to witness it. We were shaken enough by the gunfire that the thought of leaving the house could not have been further from our minds. However, we had previously made plans for just such a contingency.

According to our arrangement, in such a situation, Giuseppe and I would stay in the apartment while Rafaela, Selim, and Charlie would go to outside to film the clashes. But Giuseppe was going through training in Ramallah, so it was decided that I should stay at home alone. This was very much against ISM protocol, but Rafaela and Selim both wanted to go out, Rafaela insisting that Charlie go with her because of his experience. The fervor with which they argued was impressive, and I agreed to stay by myself.

I was somewhat relieved that I would not have to face an army possibly using live ammunition in the dead of night, where the protection offered me by my white skin and foreign appearance would not be as strong as it was during the day. However, as I sat on the couch in the living room listening to the gunfire, I began having second thoughts.

What would I do if soldiers knocked down the door? Would they shoot me just as they had so many others? Should I destroy the computers as we had discussed? Would I have enough time to do so once they were in the apartment? Should I get all my stuff together in case I was arrested and then deported?

At ISM training they told us to ensure that our phones were fully charged and had enough credit whenever we were in a situation where arrest was likely or even possible. I checked my phone. When I had traveled to Palestine the previous summer, the concierge at my hotel in Jerusalem had encouraged me to buy an Israeli simcard, as I could use it both in Israel and in the Occupied Territories. He had neglected to mention that it was much more expensive than either of the two Palestinian networks. I had lost the Palestinian simcard I had purchased later that summer, and now l had only this Israeli simcard, but it was out of credit. I had attempted to buy a Palestinian simcard in a small shop near the *Duwar*, but the owner had requested a copy of my passport. Charlie had advised me never to give my passport to a phone shop. I imagined the Israeli border officials at the airport might be able to use this information to determine that I had spent significant time in the West Bank, and I did not want to take any chances. So here I was without a working phone.

My thoughts were interrupted by loud banging on the door. I did not know what to do. My heart was beating so loudly that I was sure the soldiers could hear it. They would not really hurt me, would they? I would just explain things to them, and they would understand. After all, they were human beings. I knew of the things they did to Palestinians with regularity, but that was because they were scared. They would not be scared of me. I was in my forties, a university professor, and foreign. They could take me, arrest me, send me to prison, and then deport me if they wanted to. I just did not think I could handle being beaten by them.

I thought about whether it would be better to open the door or not. If they had to break it down, they would be even angrier. It was not like the door was going to stop them anyway; so I decided to open it.

"Sorry. I forgot the key. False alarm. The clashes weren't at the *Duwar*. They're actually in one of the camps, and we can't go there."

Charlie clapped me on the shoulder, and Rafaela and Selim followed him into the apartment. They all seemed relieved that they had not had to face the army, but I do not think they were half as relieved as I was to see them again.

***

I had trouble falling asleep. All the adrenaline from earlier in the evening had probably not yet cleared my system. Even though I had not been in any danger, I found myself glad to be alive. I was relieved to have made it through another day. I wondered if this is what soldiers felt like during a war: just happy to be alive at the end of each day.

10
Thursday, June 26
The Hares Boys

Today would be Charlie's last day in Nablus. He would travel to Ramallah with us for the biweekly financial meeting, spend the night in the ISM apartment and then attend one more demonstration on Friday before going home the next day.

He had been in Palestine for three months, almost all of that time in Nablus. He had been the coordinator of the Nablus team as well as the financial coordinator for ISM, and he had worked tirelessly as both. Only twenty-two years old, he was mature beyond his years. Most kids of that age in his home country of Spain are thinking more about drinking, chasing women or the Barcelona-Real Madrid rivalry, but Charlie focused his energies on other issues. He had been engaged in activist efforts back home, but Palestine was a different animal. Here he took on a much greater leadership role, and he had enormous responsibility in both of his coordinator jobs. From my understanding he had completely revamped ISM's accounting procedures, and as regional coordinator he had been responsible for managing all of ISM's activities in and around Nablus. And now he was leaving. It must have been difficult for him, although he did not appear overly emotional. Perhaps he was not the sentimental type.

We would be taking the *service* to Ramallah early in the afternoon, but before we left Charlie wanted to tell Selim and me about a project that lay dear to his heart.

"The Hares Boys" had been written on the whiteboard in the living room since I arrived a week earlier. I had not thought much about it, but now Charlie explained who these boys were. There were five of them. They had been in Israeli prison for over a year. Sometimes when there was a court date, ISMers would travel to the court, located in a small town north of Jenin and close to the border with Syria, in order to provide moral support to the boys and their families.

In the evening of March 14, 2013, Adva Biton, a female settler, was involved in a traffic accident on her way to the settlement of Yakir, which lies southwest of Nablus. One of Biton's three daughters sustained serious injuries, from which she died two years later. The accident, which occurred near the Palestinian village of Hares, took place when Biton crashed her car into the back of a truck that was parked along the side of the road. The driver of the truck told police that he had pulled over to repair a flat tire. There were no eyewitnesses. The problems began when Biton changed her story a few days later, claiming that the accident had been caused not by the truck but by Palestinian youths who had been throwing stones.

Despite the complete lack of evidence that a crime had occurred, the Israeli army went into action. It entered the villages of Hares and nearby Kifl Hares three times, arresting a total of nineteen boys between the ages of sixteen and seventeen years. The nighttime raids were violent, and the soldiers behaved aggressively. Accompanied by attack dogs and Israeli secret service (*Shabak*) agents, they broke down the doors of villagers' houses and demanded to know the whereabouts of all the teenage sons. They handcuffed and blindfolded the boys without telling their families why or where they were taking them.

"'Kiss and hug your mother goodbye,' a *Shabak* agent told one boy. 'You may never see her again.'"[1]

All of the boys endured violent interrogations, and they were kept in solitary confinement. "One boy, since released, described his cell: a windowless hole one meter wide and two meters long; there was no mattress or blanket to sleep on; toilet facilities were dirty; the six lights were kept on continuously, leading to the boy losing track of the time of the day; the food made him feel ill. The boy was denied a lawyer; he was interrogated violently three times during three days."[2] After this ill-treatment, fourteen of the nineteen boys were released, while five confessed to the crimes. These were the Hares boys.

Charlie's face during his telling of the Hares boys' story did not betray any emotion, but I imagined he must have been incensed, having followed these events for the past three months. He had even been to the court and later described the treatment that the boys' families and other visitors received at the hands of the authorities.[3]

I wondered if this is what happened to activists after they had been in country for a while. Did they just become accustomed to the violence and suffering and especially the injustice? Perhaps it was Charlie's defense mechanisms that allowed him to push these emotions out of his mind until he was in a place where it would be safe to let them out without being overwhelmed by them.

In the ISM training they had told us about the psychological effects of our activist experience. They had warned us that we might not notice any change in our personalities or moods while in Palestine, but that we could experience fits of rage, depression, apathy, etc. upon our return to our homes. Even in the best-case scenario we could expect a period of adjustment back to our regular lives.

The Israeli media played a significant role in the case of the Hares boys. A few days after the accident, rumors began to surface that it had been a terrorist attack, and the subsequent media storm caused sixty-one witnesses to come forward, claiming that their cars had also been damaged by stones thrown on the same road that day. Prime Minister Netanyahu himself got involved, announcing proudly that "he had caught the terrorists that did it."[4]

A report by B'Tselem indicates that the Hares boys never had a chance.[5] Between 2005 and 2010, 835 children were arrested in the West Bank on charges of stone throwing, of which only one was acquitted. Similarly, *Ha'aretz* reported that in 2010, 99.74 percent of Palestinians tried in the West Bank were convicted.[6]

The Hares boys were awaiting their fate in the notorious Meggido prison in Israel, where the conditions are reportedly atrocious, especially for minors.[7]

***

Most of the population of the West Bank has lived under military occupation for close to fifty years. Only the settlers are exempt. The lives of the Palestinians are ruled by the military and they are subject to military law, which is enforced by military courts. The system is based on military orders, which are issued by army commanders without approval from any civilian branch of government. They rule all aspects of Palestinian life in the West Bank, including freedom of movement, agriculture, access to water, ability to protest, and land transactions.

Some of these orders are patently absurd (Military Order 107 prohibits the publication of treatises on Arabic grammar), while others have far-reaching consequences. Military Order 1651, for example, allows for the incarceration of children as young as twelve years old. It also allows for the administrative detention of individuals without charge for up to six months. It is this military system that has destroyed the lives of the Hares boys and their families, as it has so many others.

On November 26, 2015, over a year after I left Palestine, the families' worst nightmares came true. The news arrived that the Hares boys were sentenced to fifteen years in prison and fined roughly $40,000 each.[8]

***

At the end of the ISM financial meeting in Ramallah, I gave Charlie a hug. He handed me the coordinator phone. The regional coordinator for each ISM team is elected by all of the members who care to vote, but in my case there was no election, since there were no other viable candidates. Selim would be leaving in a week, and Giuseppe had just completed his training, and, in addition, his English skills were sorely lacking. I became the Nablus regional coordinator by default.

In the *service* on the way back to Nablus it was too loud for conversation, so I thought about the next day's demonstration at Kufr Qaddum, a village located thirteen kilometers west of Nablus. Some of the other ISMers had told me that the protests there were particularly violent, more so than at Ni'lin, Bil'in, or Nabi Saleh. Selim and I were both anxious about it. I had come to the conclusion that the greatest chance of getting injured or even killed would be at a demonstration. I had arrived in Palestine on June 17, planning to fly back on August 11, and I calculated that there were eight Fridays between those dates. I had already survived the first Friday at Ni'lin, and now seven remained.

***

The *service* slowed down and stopped at the side of the road. The night was black and we could not see anything. A small boy, who looked like he could not have been more than four years old, clambered across his father's lap to urinate outside the van. When he finished, the occupants of the *service* all clapped and cheered. The boy climbed shyly back into the van, but his father beamed and gently stroked his son's head. I supposed it was some sort of initiation rite for a boy to take his first bathroom break in public. I congratulated the father, but the only Arabic word I knew for urinate was *'amal bibi*, a phrase uttered by small children, roughly equivalent to "make pee pee." The van erupted in laughter, but the laughter felt warm and happy, devoid of mockery. It was heartwarming.

11
Friday, June 27
Ransacking Houses in Awerta

"MAN, THE ARMY WAS IN AWERTA LAST NIGHT! They raided a bunch of homes!" I could hear the stress in Abdullah's voice over the phone.

Awerta, a village a ten-minute *service* ride from the center of Nablus, was Abdullah's hometown, and it was where he still lived in a house with his parents and sisters. His older brother Waleed was currently in prison, but he was expected to be released in a few weeks.

"I can't go to Kufr Qaddum with you guys today, and you shouldn't go by yourselves for the first time. I'm going to talk to some people in Awerta to see if you can come by to interview them. Maybe late this afternoon."

I was relieved not to be going to the demonstration at Kufr Qaddum, but I felt I was inevitably going to have to face this village at some point. On the other hand, I was happy that I would be going to Awerta and possibly helping out Abdullah.

***

The village of Awerta has a history of confrontation with the Israeli army and with the nearby Israeli settlement of Itamar. On March 11, 2011, five members of a settler family, including a four-month-old infant, were stabbed to death in the middle of the night. A trail of clues led investigators to conclude that the perpetrators had come from Awerta.

The army declared Awerta a closed military zone and placed it under curfew. They raided many of the houses in the village and, according to reports, took in all the men of Awerta for questioning.[1] There were reports of extremely aggressive behavior by the soldiers as they knocked down doors and ransacked the villagers' homes, destroying furniture in the process.[2] At one point the army arrested one hundred Palestinian women, but they were released after being questioned.[3]

Israeli authorities believe that the attack may have been in response to the murder of two teenagers from Awerta, who had been collecting garbage near Itamar.[4] Eventually the IDF arrested two cousins, who admitted to the killings and explained that they were in response to the Occupation. The young men were tried, convicted, and sentenced to five lifetimes in prison.[5]

When I asked Abdullah whether he thought the two cousins had really committed the crime, he said that he did not know. He explained that he did not know them very well, but that they were the types who had never been involved in anything political. He said that the army often arrested young children for questioning and pressured them to give them information. At that point the terrified kids would just respond with any name they could think of or sometimes even the name of someone they were currently squabbling with. Abdullah told me that the army still came into the village on a regular basis, making trouble for the residents and simply trying to make their lives as miserable as possible. He thought it was revenge for the Itamar massacre.

***

The army had entered Awerta the previous night, and Abdullah wanted us to interview some of the residents whose houses had been raided in order to file a report for ISM. Late in the afternoon, Selim and I took a *service* to the main square in the village, which lay on top of a hill and afforded splendid views of the valley below.

There were several young boys playing with a donkey in the dusty square, but they stopped when we disembarked from the van. Most of these kids had probably never seen a white man *not* in an army uniform, and I was fairly certain they had never encountered an Asian. They were even more astounded when I smiled at them and said a few words in Arabic. As I often did with children in Palestine, I asked them whether their preferred soccer hero was Messi or Ronaldo. Messi's red and blue Barcelona jersey is ubiquitous in the West Bank, but his popularity has waned slightly with the older boys because of his reputation as a Zionist. Ronaldo, by contrast, is known as pro-Palestinian and once told a reporter from Israel that he refused to answer questions from the representative of a terrorist state. I have also heard rumors that he has given large sums to charities in Gaza. I nevertheless encountered Messi's name more often here, possibly because Palestinians can identify with his status as an underdog that his modesty and diminutive physical stature provide him.

Next to the square were a large mosque and two convenience stores. Abdullah was nowhere to be seen, so we sat down in front of one of the stores to wait. After a few minutes he came running down the street with a big grin on his face.

"Welcome to Awerta!" he shouted gleefully and shook our hands warmly.

As he led us down the narrow streets to his home, dozens of passers-by greeted him, and every once in a while we were introduced to a neighbor, uncle, or cousin. A group of kids followed us, giggling and shouting. I would say a few things to them in Arabic causing them to giggle even more. There were not many women on the street, and those who were usually carried bags of groceries with a baby attached to their hips. They smiled at us as well. The few younger women I saw lowered their gaze as we approached, but I could sense them looking curiously in our direction after we passed. One of Abdullah's cousins, who appeared to be about fourteen, shook my hand happily when he was introduced, but he dutifully ran off ahead of us when Abdullah ordered him to prepare us some drinks.

There is an expression in Arabic, *kebeer el ballad*, which literally means big man of the country, and it refers to someone who is respected in his neighborhood. Judging by the number of people who greeted Abdullah, I would say he was most definitely a *kebeer el ballad* in Awerta.

We were served Coca-Cola in plastic cups by Abdullah's cousin as we sat on white plastic chairs in his back yard. It was roughly six o'clock in the evening, and we enjoyed the cool breeze as we sat under a pair of olive trees. Abdullah told us he was glad we had come to visit his house and his village. It made him extremely proud. I was anxious to talk about the events of the night before, but I knew it would be rude to change the topic of conversation abruptly. This was when Abdullah told us about his brother Waleed for the first time.

Waleed had been in prison for the last three years, but he was to be released sometime during the next few weeks. There were tears in Abdullah's eyes as he recounted the story.

"I miss him so much. He's my only brother and I have not been allowed to visit him in prison. I feel like I have to protect my sisters all by myself. But it's more than that. I haven't seen him in three years. My mom and dad have visited him twice, but it's been harder for me since I was in prison before." I wondered what crime Waleed had committed, but Abdullah said he had done nothing.

"The army came one night and raided many of the houses in the village. It was the time after the murder of that family in the settlement, when they arrested a lot of people, including children. They took me and Waleed, and they put me in prison for several months. One of the children who was taken away was forced into saying something bad about Waleed, and he got three years."

I could not imagine the gentle Abdullah in prison, but I was not surprised he had spent time there. According to the International Action Center,[6] forty percent of all male Palestinians have been incarcerated. I had many questions for Abdullah, but I let him continue with his story.

"The scariest thing for me will be when Waleed is released. Of course I'm happy, but I'm also scared. He went to prison when he was just a boy. And now he is a man. I know many people who have been released from prison, and they are so different from before. They are more serious, and they always want to be alone."

I knew that torture was rampant in Israeli prisons. According to B'Tselem, "more than eighty-five percent of Palestinians detained since 1967 have been subjected to torture, and at least 197 have died in prison."[7] I could not imagine what it must have been like for Waleed, especially when he knew the entire time that he had done nothing wrong. Of course he would be a changed man when he emerged from prison.

At that moment we were interrupted as a shy slight man in his late twenties appeared hesitantly in the backyard. Abdullah kissed him on both cheeks and invited him to sit down. Abdullah explained that Sayeed was a shop-keeper whose brother's house had been visited by soldiers the night before.

Sayeed spoke absolutely no English, and I was glad Abdullah was there to translate for us. Apparently Sayeed had received a phone call at two o'clock in the morning. Soldiers were ransacking his brother's house, which was at the other end of the village. The brother was out of town, so Sayeed quickly ran over, but he was too late to do anything other than survey the damage. The soldiers had destroyed everything. Sayeed's brother's neighbors told him that the soldiers had knocked on the door and became enraged when nobody answered. They then proceeded to destroy all they could lay their hands on. Sayeed said his brother would return the next day to try to salvage as much of his property as he could. I asked him how the soldiers' actions made him feel, but he just shrugged.

"We are used to this. It happens every so often."

***

Before we visited the house of Nadeem Suleiman, a local schoolteacher, Abdullah warned me that it was better if I did not speak Arabic in Awerta.

"People are suspicious of foreigners and, if they hear you speaking Arabic, they might think you are working for Israel."

It was hard to imagine the wonderful, welcoming people of Awerta suspecting me of being a spy, but I promised to do my best not to make the owner of the house suspicious.

The situation reminded me of a similar scenario I had encountered in Egypt in the aftermath of the revolution in 2011. After Mubarak's regime collapsed, control of the country fell to the Supreme Council of the Armed Forces, a collection of twenty or so senior army officers known as SCAF and headed by the septuagenarian Marshall Tantawi. In the first few heady weeks after the revolution there was a great deal of hope and patriotism in the air, but when real change was slow to come and the economy continued to languish, many people blamed SCAF. In a strategy many dictatorships in the Middle East had employed before them, SCAF pointed the finger at a vague network of foreign spies. They warned Egyptians to be wary of foreigners and even started a public relations campaign to discredit them. There was a very popular television commercial that featured a supposedly Western individual trying to befriend Egyptians in a café. He asked questions about military equipment and secretly sent the responses to his bosses on his cell phone. The message of the commercial was clear, but in case it was missed by the viewer, at the end the narrator concluded with a warning.

"Mind what you say carefully! Every word has a price! A word can save a nation."

I believed that the popularity of the commercial stemmed from its absurdity, as was confirmed to me by many of my Egyptian friends. But there were people who took heed of its message, especially in areas of the country not frequented by tourists. The commercial's success in spreading SCAF's anti-foreigner rhetoric could be evidenced by the fact that the actor who played the foreigner, himself an Egyptian, was subsequently beaten up by a mob.

The commercial was being aired during the run-up to the first round of the presidential elections. It was to be the first free election in Egyptian history, and the entire country was obsessed with it. It was essentially a referendum on two systems of government—the old guard and army on one hand—and the Muslim Brotherhood with its Islamic views on the other.

One of my best friends at that time was Ibrahim, my Arabic tutor, and he invited me to come with him as he went to vote. Although he now lived in Maadi, a well-to-do suburb of Cairo, he was registered in Shubra al-Kheima, a poor neighborhood where he had grown up and where his family still lived. As we took a *tuktuk*, a three-wheeled open air taxi, from the metro station to the school where Ibrahim was supposed to vote, I took pictures. I had been to Shubra only once before, and I found this neighborhood, with its high-rise buildings covered with advertising from top to bottom, fascinating.

As we turned a corner near the school, somebody rapped on the roof of the taxi and demanded that I turn over my camera. I refused and a commotion ensued. After a minute or so, we were surrounded by a mob of people, some of whom were trying to grab my camera. I remember an older woman begging me to just hand over my camera so I would not get hurt. I could see that Ibrahim was afraid, and I knew the situation was serious. Eventually we convinced one of the older men in the mob to join us in the taxi, and we drove for about a hundred meters, so I could show him the pictures in my camera. Realizing that I was not in fact a spy, the old man apologized as did a few of the others from the mob who had been chasing the taxi. I was unhurt but a little shaken by the incident.

***

In the living room of the house of Nadeem Suleiman, there were roughly ten men as well as two boys sitting with us. The men were angry, and even the boys looked very serious. There were no pleasantries or idle banter. These men, most of whom were smoking, were anxious to get down to business. Nadeem told us what had happened the previous night.

At midnight approximately fifteen soldiers had entered his home and demanded that he show them the location of his guns. Were he not to obey, he could be confident that the house would be destroyed. Nadeem replied that Israeli soldiers had already been to his house many times and had never found anything. He had no guns, he assured them.

A heavy-set man sitting next to Nadeem interrupted him angrily.

"He's a schoolteacher. Why would he have guns? It's ridiculous. They just want to fuck with us. And America just lets it happen. Democracy? America talks about democracy, and this is what they do. Is this what they mean by democracy?"

I wondered what made the soldiers believe there might be guns in the house, and I asked Abdullah to find out from Nadeem, but he gave me a look that seemed to say, "There is no reason. The soldiers don't need a reason. They just assume every Arab is a terrorist."

The soldiers blindfolded and handcuffed Nadeem's twenty-year-old son and took him outside for an interrogation that lasted three hours. They herded the rest of the family, which included an eight-month-old baby and several other children, into the living room. Again they asked Nadeem about his guns.

"Watch what we will do if you don't give them to us!" an officer yelled. The children listened in terror as the soldiers proceeded to ransack the house. They ripped apart sofas and chairs, threw the contents of shelves on the floor, knocked over electrical appliances, destroyed two computers, and slashed the family's water tank on the roof.

In Palestine many houses get their water from a tank that sits on the roof. The soldiers knew that this was the only source of water for the whole family. Why did they destroy it? It could only have been to make life difficult for the family. Although I had seen plenty of evidence of abhorrent behavior such as this from Israeli soldiers, it still shocked me. The soldiers were human beings, were they not? What made one group of humans do this to another group of humans?

The entire family had now been sitting in the living room for several hours, and by this point it was unbearably hot. The children were complaining and Nadeem begged the soldiers to allow the baby a drink, but this request was denied. Sometime during the night, Nadeem's thirteen-year-old son was taken outside the living room and interrogated for half an hour. A soldier held his rifle to the boy's face and demanded the location of the guns. He held a piece of cloth to the boy's mouth until he became dizzy.

"It was probably chloroform," Nadeem said angrily. "How could they do this to Hossam? He's just a kid. They held a gun to his head! What kind of person does something like that? Is he not human?"

As I looked at Hossam, who was sitting on his father's armrest, I wondered the same thing. What kind of person was this soldier? I wish I could have asked him. The look on Hossam's face was heartbreaking. He was obviously still terrified by the events of the night. What kind of man would Hossam be when or if he grew up? How could he not be consumed by rage, itching to get revenge on the people who humiliated and oppressed him and his family on a daily basis? Even if he never committed any crime, there was a good chance that he would spend at least some time in prison. What would he be like once he got out?

The soldiers finished searching the house, having found no weapons. They released both of Nadeem's sons and left the house at approximately four o'clock in the morning.

"And what is going to happen now?" shouted the man sitting next to

Nadeem. "Nothing. Who will pay for all the damage these soldiers did? We will clean up, and they will come back next month and do the same thing all over again."

I assured him that ISM would publish a report about the raid, including the part about the soldiers drugging a thirteen-year-old with chloroform. There was not much else we could do. People would see the report, and most of them would become angry and appalled by the injustice. Some of them would do something about it. Maybe they would go to demonstrations or stop buying Israeli products at the supermarket. Maybe they would write their congressperson and demand that the US government take action. It would take time, but eventually something would happen. It was the same with the Apartheid regime in South Africa. It took time, but eventually the international pressure was strong enough to cause the regime to collapse. It was true that there was not much in the way of pressure right now in the case of Israel, but things were changing. On November 29, 2012, Palestine had been granted observer status at the UN, which meant they could take Israel to the ICJ.[8] The Boycott, Divestment, and Sanctions movement had slowly become more and more effective.[9] These were small gains, to be sure, but the momentum was there.

I was sure none of these men felt particularly hopeful at this time, and I did not blame them. Their country had been under a brutal military occupation for close to fifty years, and things had only been deteriorating for most of that time. But what else could people do but hope?

***

I was feeling despondent when we left the house of the schoolteacher. Abdullah took us to his grandmother's house, which was on the road from Awerta back to Nablus. She was ninety years old, but she looked to be even older. She lived in the one-room house with only a tiny kitten for a companion. It was clear that Abdullah adored her and that she reveled in his love. She was almost entirely deaf and, whenever Abdullah wanted to say something to her, he had to shout. She laughed uproariously every time he said anything to her, including when he explained who Selim and I were. As the four of us sat on her front porch, the kitten bounded back and forth between us happily.

After a few minutes one of Abdullah's best friends joined us. Hany looked like a young Sylvester Stallone, and his open smile made me feel a connection to him right away. He looked like he spent at least a few hours in the gym every day, and Abdullah would make fun of him by pretending not to be able to wrap his arms around one of Hany's biceps. We spent another half an hour at Abdullah's grandmother's house, but it was well past midnight by now, so Abdullah called one of his friends to take us home to Nablus.

12
Saturday, June 28
Ramadan

I SPENT THE MORNING WRITING UP MY REPORT on the raids in Awerta and sent it to Cynthia in Ramallah to be published. In the afternoon Abdullah came by the apartment, which he did on occasion even if there was not any work to be done. He and I sat in the kitchen as he told me about his dreams. It was a hot day, and he was wearing jeans and a white undershirt. He usually had a goatee, and he looked like he had not shaved the rest of his face in a few days. We were sitting in plastic chairs, and he was leaning back in his, so far back that I thought he might fall, but he rested against the refrigerator. As he sucked on his cigarette, he blew the smoke out the kitchen window and spoke softly.

"Life is shit here, man." That was the standard beginning to all of his stories about his life, and I had heard it from him many times before.

"Look at this fucking cigarette, man. Cigarettes used to be cheap, but the PA has raised the prices. Now it costs me twenty-five shekels a day to smoke. It is one of the few pleasures I have in life. I only make sixty shekels a day in my job, and I have to spend twenty-five on cigarettes." I asked him if he thought he was addicted.

"No. I can quit any time I want to. I've quit many times before, but there really isn't any point. Smoking is the only thing I look forward to."

"You know, Abdullah, if you keep smoking like this, you're going to get sick. And you won't be able to take care of your family if you get really ill. But think about this. Your dream is to travel to Europe, right? If you stop smoking, that is twenty-five shekels every day you'll save. That's 750 shekels a month, which translates to 9,000 shekels a year. Do you know how much money that is? You could fly anywhere in Europe that you want and still have money left over." I could see I had piqued Abdullah's interest, but he was still hesitant.

"If I don't spend the money on cigarettes, then I'll spend it on something else. I just can't help myself." But I had an idea.

"Ramadan starts tomorrow. That means you can't smoke during the day anyway. It will be easier for you to quit. But here's the deal. I will fast for the whole month, and you will stop smoking." Abdullah laughed and claimed that there was no way I would be able to fast for that long, so it would not matter. Sure, he would agree to the deal.

***

According to Islamic tradition, the prophet Muhammad first began receiving divine revelations during the lunar month of Ramadan. The celebration of Ramadan is one of the five pillars of Islam and is considered to be obligatory for all Muslims, who are required to abstain from eating, drinking, smoking, and sexual activity between sunrise and sunset. Some people, such as the ill, travelers, and women who are pregnant or menstruating, are exempt from these requirements. Muslims are expected to spend time reading the Qur'an, praying, and reflecting on their relationship with God. It is also a time to celebrate with one's family and friends. One of the purposes of the fast is to ensure that everyone can understand what it feels like to be hungry and thirsty. It increases empathy with those on the margins of society. During Ramadan it is customary for the rich to give money and food to the poor.

At night many Palestinians have huge feasts with their families and friends. They count the hours until sunset, which is announced by the *muezzin* in every mosque, and then they begin with the feast. Usually people will wake up before sunrise to have another meal before they go back to bed and try to sleep for a bit longer.

Because Ramadan is based on the lunar calendar, it can occur at any time of the solar year. Thus it can present an enormous variety of challenges depending on the time and location. For example, the long days during the summer months in northern countries can make fasting more difficult. My first experience with Ramadan was in Cairo in September of 2010. It is always hot in Egypt that time of year, but that particular summer was brutal. For many people the most difficult part of Ramadan is not being able to drink. This year Ramadan would run the entire month of July, when the weather would be very hot in Palestine.

It is considered rude to eat or drink in front of someone who is fasting during Ramadan, although locals generally will not say anything if you forget and take a quick sip of water. The previous Ramadan our Arabic professor at Birzeit told us he had no problem if we wanted to drink in front of him. I have been told the same thing by many people over my years of travel in the Middle East. But some Muslims are more sensitive about this than others. Later in the month I witnessed Steve, a British ISMer, being admonished that his behavior was extremely disrespectful when he forgot where he was and noisily ate a chocolate bar on the street.

My German friend Klaus, who was a classmate at Birzeit, decided to fast in solidarity with his Muslim friends. He would show up to class looking exhausted and miserable. He was taking five hours of Arabic every day at that time, and he usually would skip the second class. I knew that he lived a twenty-minute walk from campus, and I could picture him struggling to climb up the steep hill to his house in the burning noonday sun before dragging himself to bed. I remember that he lasted about two weeks before he finally gave up.

I could never truly identify with the suffering of Palestinians, but what I could do is share in it a little. Just like many Palestinians, I had been tear-gassed and shot at by Israeli soldiers, but after all was said and done, I could leave. I knew I could always go home to my regular life. That knowledge alone set me apart, but perhaps fasting was a way in which I could stand in greater solidarity with the people in Palestine. I did not think it would be that difficult for me, and now that I had that extra incentive with Abdullah's promise that he would stop smoking if I succeeded, I had full confidence that I would make it through the whole month.

All the talk of Ramadan in the kitchen of the ISM apartment led to a discussion of religion in general. Abdullah was a devout Muslim, and during the day he would often perform *wudu*, the ritual cleansing, before taking his prayer rug into one of the bedrooms to face Mecca and pray. Like many devout Muslims that I had encountered, he would often try to convince me that the way of Islam constituted the only true path in life, and we ended up having many long conversations about the topic.

13
Sunday, June 29
Khan al-Lubban

T HE LAND AND SPRING AT KHAN AL-LUBBAN have belonged to the extended family of Khalid al-Sanih Daraghmah for generations, and in 2007 he bought the existing two buildings on the property from his cousin with the hopes of restoring them and planting the land. In 2002 the Israeli Supreme Court had ordered that the spring belonged to the family, but Israeli settlers had other ideas, claiming that it was on public land. In the first six months after Khalid purchased the buildings, Israeli real estate agents approached him with offers to buy the property. When it became clear that he would not sell, the settlers of nearby Ma'ale Levona began using more direct methods: cutting down trees on the property, stealing food, and using water from the spring. Eventually the settlers set one of the two buildings on fire, and Khalid was forced to move his family into the other house. Two years later, in 2010, after several more attacks on his property, he decided it was too dangerous to live there, so most of his family left. Only Khalid and his two eldest sons remained to work the land and protect the property. In the following years ISM documented several more extremely violent actions by both settlers and the Israeli army that caused serious injury to Khalid and his family.[1]

On occasion, when an ISM team had sufficient manpower and when the situation merited it, we would send a couple of people to stay overnight with a Palestinian family. This was done when the family thought there was a good chance that it was going to be attacked by the Israeli army or by settlers. In the case of an army attack, our presence would hopefully dissuade the soldiers from behaving as violently as they might otherwise, especially if we were filming them. It was not clear to me how settlers would react once they saw that there were ISMers on the Palestinian family's property. Settlers seem less concerned with their image vis-à-vis the international community and, in fact, they have attacked and injured international activists, including ISMers, on numerous occasions.

***

It was three o'clock in the afternoon, and the sun was beating down on us mercilessly as we waited by the side of the road for a *service* to take us back to Nablus. I was exhausted, not having eaten or drunk anything since before sunrise, roughly ten hours earlier. It seemed that Ramadan was going to be a very difficult experience for me.

Selim and I had spent the day in Khan al-Lubban to determine if Khalid required an ISM presence in the near future, but he demurred, explaining that settlers were usually less violent during Ramadan. I had been overwhelmed by the strength that Khalid projected. He was not a large man, and his fortitude came from elsewhere. On his own he had faced down settlers and soldiers alike for many years now. What kind of strength was required to continue fighting and resisting the way he did?

For an hour we attempted to flag down a *service* but to no avail. They all appeared to be full. There was a village a few kilometers up the main road, and we decided to walk in that direction while checking for *services*. The hours of fasting—and especially not drinking—in the hot sun had taken their toll, and by this time all I wanted to do was drink a big bottle of beautiful ice-cold Coca-Cola and lie down in a shady spot. That would have to wait until we arrived back in Nablus, which was probably not going to happen any time soon. After we walked for thirty minutes, a car slowed down beside us to drop off a passenger. I was getting desperate now.

"Excuse me," I asked the driver, a young man. "Could you tell us how to find a *service* to Nablus?"

"Why don't I just give you a lift? I'm not going all the way to Nablus, but I'm going in the same direction. At least you'll be closer."

I hesitated. All my life I had been imbued with the North American idea that only those with a death wish would risk hitchhiking. I thought about the three teenaged settlers who had been kidnapped recently near Hebron. They had been hitchhiking. But in the end our thirst and fatigue won out, and we gratefully got into the car, deeply inhaling the wonderful cool air inside.

I looked at the driver, a well-dressed and clean-cut young man in his early twenties. His name was Amr.

"It's not often that you see foreigners standing by the side of the road in Palestine. Did your car break down?" Amr asked us.

"We took a *service* to Khan al-Lubban, and we are trying to get back home to Nablus. But all the *services* seem to be full." Amr looked at me quizzically.

"It's a couple of buildings near al-Lubban esh-Sharqiya," I replied to his unasked question. "We were investigating the troubles the residents are having with the settlers."

Amr told us he was from Awerta, the same village that Abdullah lived in and that we had visited just a few days earlier. I had forgotten Abdullah's last name, but after I mentioned Hany, Abdullah's Sylvester Stallone look-a-like friend, and flexed my muscles just to make things clearer, Amr said he knew whom I was talking about.

"I don't know Abdullah well, but I know who he is. If he is from Awerta, then I consider you to be from Awerta as well. I cannot give you a ride all the way to Nablus, but my father's shop is on the road close to Nablus. He will give you a ride."

I thought about protesting against this overly generous act, but I just did not have the energy, and based on my history with Palestinian hospitality, I knew that Amr would have insisted anyway. I thanked him for his kindness and settled back to enjoy the comfort of the front seat and the air conditioning, secure in the knowledge that I would soon be home.

After fifteen minutes Amr stopped the car and got out in front of an auto mechanic's garage.

"My father will be right back to take you to Nablus," he said as he bounded away.

"Thank you! Thank you!" I shouted after him.

A minute later a man in his fifties opened the driver's side door and sat down. He beamed at us and shook hands with us heartily.

"I'm Aziz. Amr is my son. I will take you from here." We tried to protest and said we would find a taxi to take us the rest of the way, but Aziz insisted.

"I'm a taxi driver. And that's what you want, isn't it? Amr told me about the work you are doing here. Anybody that wants to help Palestine is a friend of mine."

The Israeli occupation of Palestine is pervasive. It affects the life of almost every Palestinian, and Aziz was no exception.

According to a 2010 report issued by the British *Middle East Monitor*, roughly 40,000 residents of the West Bank work in Israel. Approximately 17,000 of these do not have a permit to do so, and they must enter and exit Israel illegally.[2]

Aziz used to drive some of these men from a meeting point near Nablus to the border with Israel, where they would then cross illegally. On one of the excursions Aziz was apprehended by the police, and although he himself had not crossed the border, he was arrested. He was placed under house arrest for one-and-a-half years and fined 40,000 shekels, an enormous amount for someone of his limited means. The house arrest meant that he was unable to work.

"They come here and steal our land. Then they steal more. And when they've stolen almost everything, they try to destroy what little we have left.

Our economy is in shambles. There is so much unemployment. What are we supposed to do? We have to feed our families, so some people go to Israel. They have no choice."

Aziz said the worst thing about his arrest was not being able to care for his loved ones.

"When the Israelis arrest you, you're not the only one who suffers. Your whole family bears the brunt of it. It's especially bad if the bread winner of the family is arrested. How is the family supposed to survive?"

As we approached Nablus, we passed the intersection of the main highway with another road that led to a settlement in the hills. There were several bus shelters near the intersection, at one of which I saw two settlers waiting. It was a young man and woman in their early twenties. He was wearing shorts and a t-shirt, and he was sporting the traditional Jewish *payot*, or side locks. On his head he was wearing a *kippa*, the traditional Jewish "hat" worn by men as a sign of respect for God. His companion was wearing a long skirt and the scarf that I had seen so many conservative Jewish women wear at the Wailing Wall in Jerusalem. At another of the shelters were two soldiers, presumably there to protect the settlers.

It was a scene that I witnessed on several occasions, and it never failed to fascinate me. The settlers appeared at ease, but they must have known that almost every single person driving along this road hated them. I wondered what it was like for them. Perhaps they had grown up here and were used to it by now.

Aziz was upbeat and optimistic when he dropped us off near the *Duwar* in Nablus.

"Thank you so much for being here and for helping Palestine!" he shouted as he sped away.

By the time Selim and I arrived back at the apartment it was five o'clock in the afternoon. Abdullah was there, sitting in front of the computer in the living room, and I flashed him the thumbs-up sign, showing him I still had not eaten or drunk anything today. I did not want to show him how weak I felt, and I tried to smile enthusiastically, but I was sure he could see right through my act. I was comforted to see that he was not looking so hot himself.

It had been a rough day both physically and emotionally, and I wanted to rest. Sunset was going to be at around 7:30, and I had only a few hours of fasting left. I thought it would be best to try to get some sleep.

I lay down on my mattress and closed my eyes, but sleep was elusive. I could not stop thinking about Khalid Daraghmah and his stand against the Israeli settlers and soldiers at Khan al-Lubban. I did not understand the settlers' behavior. Did they truly believe that they had a right to Khalid's land because their holy book said it belonged to Jews? A part of me had always believed that any two human beings would understand each other if they could just communicate. What would one of these settlers say if I asked them about Khan al-Lubban? Did he truly, in the depths of his heart, think it was acceptable to attack and beat Khalid and his family? Sometimes I thought that if I could just talk to them, I would understand.

Until that point my only interaction with Israeli settlers had taken place the previous summer at a demonstration just outside the village of Bil'in. The protesters in Bil'in had begun demonstrating against the Israeli plan of building a section of the Apartheid Wall on village land, thereby annexing part of the land to a nearby settlement. The demonstrations, as depicted in the film *Five Broken Cameras*, are violent at times, and on most occasions Israeli soldiers fire teargas and sometimes rubber bullets and even live ammunition at the protesters. It was during one of these demonstrations that villager Bassem Abu Rahmeh, whose picture is now on a poster near the village entrance, was killed when he was struck by a teargas canister.

During the demonstration I attended in June of 2013, the protesters were approaching the Wall that here separated the village of Bil'in from the settlement. On the other side were Israeli soldiers as well as about twenty settlers. The settlers were waiving enormous Israeli flags, and it seemed to me that they were mocking the Palestinians. Most of them were wearing shorts, relaxing in lawn chairs, and blaring music on loudspeakers. Every once in a while one of them would pick up a megaphone and shout obscenities at the protesters, calling them terrorists, and daring them to throw rocks at them. Two or three of the protesters, teenaged boys wearing *keffiyehs* to cover their faces, began picking up stones from the ground and using slingshots to hurl them towards the settlers.

I had heard about the slingshots, but this was my first time seeing them in action. I was shocked at their ineffectiveness, as most of the stones launched with them fell far short of their intended targets. The bigger and heavier the stone, the shorter its trajectory, and since the settlers were a safe distance away, the chances of any of them being hit was most likely miniscule. It seemed more than a little absurd to me that these settlers were acting as the tough guy when they were protected by soldiers wielding advanced and powerful weapons, while the Palestinians had nothing but a few homemade slingshots.

The soldiers responded to the slingshots by firing a barrage of teargas,

Protester with slingshot at Nabi Saleh.

causing most of the protesters to run. Some of the teenagers continued throwing stones, which evoked the firing of yet more teargas. After an hour of this back-and-forth, most of the participants on both sides of the Wall tired of this activity, and the demonstration slowly came to a halt.

On some level the whole exercise seemed surreal to me. The protesters marched to the Wall and threw stones that had no chance of hurting anybody. The soldiers fired teargas at these demonstrators, who were a threat to nobody. I could understand that the villagers merely wanted to show that they still existed, that they were not going to simply lie down and take the theft of their land unopposed. I knew why the soldiers were there: to show the Palestinians that resistance was futile, that they were so strong that it was in the Palestinians' best interest to just give up.

But why were the settlers at the demonstration? Was it merely to mock the villagers and throw it in their face that they had stolen their land? I remembered one settler who remained until the end of the demonstration, a bearded young man wearing shorts, defiantly waiving an Israeli flag and holding his fingers in a V-shape indicating victory.

I have always been confused about the naming of the Israeli-Palestinian conflict. The word *conflict* has a connotation that the involved parties are of

Palestinian protester and Israeli settlers at Bil'in.

relatively equal strength. Nobody refers to the Holocaust as the Nazi-Jewish conflict or the colonization of the Americas as the European-Native American conflict. In this situation Israel has all the power and does whatever it wants, and the Palestinians attempt to resist, and every once in a while they score a victory, if only in the arena of public opinion. This is no conflict, and there is no victory when Israel imposes its will and builds a wall on land it has occupied. Did the settler really think that he had "won" this demonstration? It would be like the Harlem Globetrotters celebrating wildly after humiliating a high school team.

***

Mingled with these thoughts about the settlers was my now near-constant obsession with my thirst. Then I decided I had had enough; it was over. The whole reason for my fasting, apart from my own ego and the confidence that I could do it, was to stand in solidarity with the Palestinians. Yet when I thought about writing a report on our visit to Khan al-Lubban in my current state, I decided I could be much more useful to the Palestinian cause by breaking my fast and continuing to work.

Every once in while I look back on this decision, and I know that it was at least in part a rationalization. I still wonder if I have the fortitude necessary to fast for an entire month, not having made it through even a single day.

Like a defeated man I walked into the kitchen and downed a two-liter bottle of Coke. It felt absolutely wonderful. At that point Abdullah wandered into the kitchen, and he laughed when he saw me.

"I knew you wouldn't be able to do it! Not even one day?! And you were talking about a whole month! I'm sure going to enjoy smoking tonight!" I smiled at my friend and shook his hand warmly.

"Ramadan *kareem*," I said to him.

14
Monday, June 30
May God Avenge their Blood

IN THE EVENING THE ISRAELI ARMY announced that it had discovered the bodies of the three teenagers who had been missing since June 12. They were found under a pile of rocks in a field near Hebron.

The authorities had known soon after their disappearance that the boys were already dead, but they kept this knowledge from the public. Instead, they had used the "search" for the boys as an excuse to mete out collective punishment on the population of the West Bank during the past three weeks. According to reports, over 400 Palestinians were arrested in the West Bank,[1] and five Palestinians, including children, were killed.[2]

I knew, however, that Israel's thirst for revenge was not to be slaked easily and that there would be more violence after the discovery of the bodies.

"Israel's Prime Minister Benjamin Netanyahu said that the teenagers 'were kidnapped and murdered in cold blood by wild beasts,'" the Associated Press reported.[3] He added: "Vengeance for the blood of a small child, Satan has not yet created. Neither has vengeance for the blood of three pure youths, who were on their way home to meet their parents, who will not see them anymore. Hamas is responsible—and Hamas will pay."[4]

Netanyahu was not the only Israeli official to make comments of this sort, as current and former lawmakers competed with him and with each other in making vitriolic and hateful statements. Some of them were collected by the *Electronic Intifada*.[5]

Back in December of 2011 a shocking video received a great deal of attention in Egypt and around the world. The revolution of January 25 in Egypt had left the Supreme Council of the Armed Forces (SCAF) in power after former President Mubarak was ousted. SCAF, which consisted of army generals, was supposed to ensure that Egypt underwent a smooth transition to democracy, but most Egyptians felt that its true objective was to hold onto power. As a result, the demonstrations at Tahrir Square and elsewhere in the country continued, and in some cases they were brutally suppressed by the military.

The video in question showed a man desperately trying to drag the lifeless body of an *abaya*-clad woman away from dozens of soldiers who were chasing them. The man was caught, and the soldiers began to beat him and the unconscious body of the woman with batons. The man was by now on the ground, simply trying to protect his head as the soldiers were raining down blows upon it. This went on for several seconds, and at the same time the soldiers were kicking the head of the woman with their heavy boots. As one soldier began to drag her away, presumably to arrest her, her shirt fell open, and her blue bra was revealed. This image of the soldier with his boot above the exposed torso of the "blue bra girl" later became a rallying cry against the abuses and excesses of military power. Another soldier leapt in the air and landed on her exposed chest with his boots.

The video was troubling for me because it showed the absolute savagery of the soldiers. They were beating the protesters not to subdue them or because they felt threatened by them, but because they were filled with rage. They did not stop. They just kept swinging their batons and kicking, trying to hurt them as much as they could, even after the woman fell unconscious. I did not understand how there could be so much anger and hatred in a person to motivate behavior like that.

The statements of Netanyahu and some of the other Israeli politicians reminded me of this video. It was clear that they truly hated the Arabs. It was also clear that they were speaking to a populace that largely agreed with them. It frightened me, and it made me extremely fearful about what was going to happen next.

In one of the first acts after the discovery of the bodies, the Israeli army demolished the homes of the two Palestinians it suspected of being behind the murder of the settlers.[6] In years past Israel used to engage in punitive home demolitions, but it had stopped, perhaps because of international pressure. However, it had recently announced that it would again use the practice, which has been outlawed by the Geneva Conventions.[7]

The IDF's escalation of punitive actions made me believe that worse was yet to come. According to *Al Jazeera*, the army had already begun bombing Gaza.[8]

15
Wednesday, July 2
Price Tag Attack

I WOKE UP TO THE NEWS OF THE MURDER OF A TEENAGER in the northern West Bank city of Jenin. Israeli soldiers had killed the sixteen-year-old Palestinian Yusuf Abu Zhaga during the invasion of a refugee camp in Jenin. They had shot him in the chest. The killing of Palestinians in refugee camps was not an uncommon occurrence, but the timing of it worried me. It had taken place on the day of the funerals of the three abducted Israeli teenagers.

Many prominent Israeli politicians, including Benjamin Netanyahu himself, had made comments on the day the bodies were found, whose only purpose seemed to me to stir up anti-Arab sentiments throughout the country. Hundreds of extremists had taken to the streets shouting "Death to Arabs" on that day. A Facebook page named "People of Israel Demand Revenge" had 35,000 likes before it was removed.[1] It was hard not to see the connection between the anti-Arab rhetoric and this most recent murder. I feared that Abu Zhaga would only be the first of many more victims.

The administrator of a popular Facebook group, many of whose members were soldiers and which garnered 70,000 likes, shared a photo of the bloodied body of Abu Zhaga with the caption "this is the terrorist we killed in Jenin last night." Almost all of the 200 comments regarding the photo were supportive.[2]

***

In the afternoon, Abdullah, Selim and I were in a *service* on our way to the village of Aqaba. After a thirty-minute drive we were dropped off at the main square in the center of town. The day was hot, and it seemed like the entire town had been shut down for Ramadan. Abdullah called his contact, but there was no answer. Presumably he was sleeping to avoid the early afternoon sun.

"I don't know anyone else here. And I have no idea where the attack happened. We just have to wait for Bakir to answer his phone, even if it takes hours," Abdullah said softly, the exhaustion caused by fasting and the heat clearly visible in his face.

We found a small shop that was open, and we asked the owner, a short and extremely fat young man, if he knew where the previous night's attack had taken place.

"There was an attack? Do you mean settlers or soldiers? There were many soldiers in Aqaba in the middle of the night, and they arrested two men. I have not heard of any attack."

Sitting next to the shop owner in a rocking chair was an old man who, judging by his appearance, was probably closely related to the owner. His eyes were closed, and I assumed he had been sleeping, but he now spoke up.

"Yes, Mansour's house was attacked last night. Show them where it is, Kazem." He gestured towards a small boy who had been kicking a soccer ball against the steps leading up to the shop when we arrived but had been curiously watching us from behind the door.

Kazem pointed in the direction of a steep hill.

"Go up there and then it's at the top of the next hill after that. It will take you half an hour if you walk fast."

Walk fast? I felt bad for Abdullah. It must have been rough for him. Not only was he fasting, which made the long trek in the heat difficult, but what did he have to look forward to at Mansour's house? For Selim and me, demonstrations and attacks were still an experience outside our normal world but, whatever awaited us, Abdullah had seen it before. These were his people, and their suffering reminded him of his own.

I often wondered why he did so much work for ISM. Did he not experience enough violence and injustice in his own life?

"It's for my people. I want to help my people," he would always tell me. But I guessed it was more than that. It felt like he was seeking a connection with a part of the world that was not filled with suffering. He wanted to know that it was possible to live a life without fear and injustice. Perhaps spending time with us even allowed him to live it temporarily. Maybe it gave him the hope that one day he could attain the freedom that we ourselves, as Westerners, seemed to take for granted.

After fifteen minutes of trudging up the hill, we were rescued by an empty *service*, which took us the rest of the way to the house of Hassim Mansour, where we disembarked.

Hassim Mansour was a farmer whose house and land lay at the edge of the village, only a hundred meters from the highway. This location presumably made it an attractive target for attacks since escape by the culprits would be much easier.

Mansour was about fifty years old with streaks of grey visible throughout his otherwise black hair. His eyes were bright with anger. He told us his story.

He lived with his extended family of fifteen in a single-room house which had an attached barn that housed his sheep. Behind the main house was another structure that he was building to house his large family but which was not yet ready for habitation.

The night before, at three o'clock, he was awakened by the sound of footsteps outside his house. When he went to investigate, he saw four men running away in the darkness. Turning back, he smelled smoke and realized that his barn, adjacent to the house, was on fire.

Mansour roused his family, and they spent the next four hours dousing the flames and rescuing the sheep from the barn. There were two large water tanks nearby, and the family was able to extinguish the fire.

"We were very lucky," Mansour explained. "Without the water tanks we would have lost everything. We had to put out the fire before any of the sheep were killed. Even before it was out completely, we went in and carried the sheep out one by one. It was brutally hot. But we saved the sheep. And then we had to worry about the house. What if the fire spread from the barn to the house? We were lucky."

Mansour walked with us to the back of the house to show us the remains of the barn. It had consisted of three wooden walls (the fourth wall was one of the stone walls of the house), a tin roof, and several metal posts that held up the roof. We could see that the wooden walls were gone and that the stone wall was blackened by the fire. The roof was still being supported by the metal posts, but other than that the barn had been completely destroyed.

"We will rebuild it," Mansour said in response to my unasked question. "We have no choice. Whatever they do, we will always rebuild. But come with me. I want to show you something else." He led us to the other side of the house, to the building under construction.

"We saw this this morning, as soon as it was light out." Spray painted on the side of one of the walls of the building were big blue Hebrew letters, roughly one square foot each. At the time I did not understand the precise meaning of the graffiti, but it was obvious to me what had happened. Extremist Jewish settlers had come here in the night and perpetrated this attack. They had burned down the barn belonging to the Mansour family, possibly attempted to burn down the house and then fled after defacing this wall.

Mansour told me he was unsure whether this crime had been committed by soldiers or settlers. I was incredulous. The crazy ones were the settlers, not the soldiers. I knew many soldiers were racists who hated the Arabs, but I could not imagine them actually burning down Palestinian houses in the middle of the night. They were supposed to be well trained, and they were supposed to follow orders.

"There were many footprints on the ground near the shed, but they were all identical, indicating that the people who did this were wearing the same kind of boots. That tells me they were soldiers. And we know the army was here last night, because they made those arrests."

I was not sure whether I agreed with him that the evidence pointed towards the soldiers, but I assumed it was possible he was right. Some of the soldiers were probably fanatical settlers. What would stop them from carrying out an attack of this kind? Somehow it was more disturbing to think of the army as being behind this act.

I found out later that day that the graffiti on the house read *Price tag, revenge of the Jews.*

Price tag attack graffiti at Aqaba, near Nablus.

According to the *New York Times*,[3] a price tag attack is an incident in which extremist Jewish settlers "exact a price from local Palestinians or from the Israeli security forces for any action taken against their settlement enterprise." Others have written that attacks perpetrated as retribution for

Palestinian violence against settlers should also be labeled price tag attacks.[4] The general idea is that if the Israeli government performs an action that is seen in any way as harmful to settlers, such as the demolition of structures in the settlements, then an immediate and steep price needs to be paid either by the government itself, or most often, by the Palestinians.

According to the Israeli newspaper *Ha'aretz*, the policy can be traced back to 2005 when the Israeli government unilaterally decided to dismantle all of the settlements in the Gaza Strip.

"The policy's roots lie in the August 2005 disengagement from Gaza and the subsequent destruction of nine houses in the West Bank outpost of Amona about six months later.

"Ever since then, the extreme right has sought to establish a 'balance of terror,' in which every state action aimed at them—from demolishing a caravan in an outpost to restricting the movements of those suspected of harassing Palestinian olive harvesters—generates an immediate, violent reaction.

"Even if this reaction cannot stop an evacuation, the theory goes, the damage it causes—whether the victims are Palestinians or Israel Defense Forces soldiers—will cause the government to think twice before ordering additional evacuations."[5]

B'Tselem has documented many price tag attacks, "including the blocking of roads, throwing stones at cars and houses, making incursions into Palestinian villages and land, torching fields, uprooting trees, and other damage to property."[6]

The Israeli government, including Prime Minister Benjamin Netanyahu, has heavily criticized price tag attacks. In 2011 Israeli President Shimon Peres, visiting a mosque that had been burned down in such an attack, stated "it is unconscionable that a Jew would harm something that is holy to another religion. . . We will not allow extremists and criminals to undercut the need to live together equally in equality and mutual respect."[7]

Despite the government's denunciations of price tag attacks, its actions often do not suffice to deter the settlers from engaging in violence. In fact, on occasion, its reaction to a price tag attack will be to punish the local Palestinian population. For example, in 2011 settlers threw stones at Palestinian cars near Nablus in reaction to the killing of a Jew by Palestinian policemen. Rather than protect the Palestinians, which it is obligated to do as an occupying power, the army forbade the locals from using a nearby road.[8]

It is difficult to find precise statistics on the number of price tags attacks throughout the West Bank, but the amount of press the issue received early in 2014 indicates that it is on the rise.[9] A particularly troubling aspect is that very few of the perpetrators are ever brought to justice.[10] One of the main reasons for this is thought to be the fact that price tag attacks are classified as crimes, rather than acts of terrorism, which makes prosecution more difficult.[11]

***

After dinner we were all hanging out in the living room: Rafaela, Giuseppe, Selim, Cathy (a colleague of Rafaela's from the International Women's Peace Service who was also staying in the ISM apartment), and me. Rafaela was in her usual spot, sitting on the floor and leaning against the living room wall with her laptop when she suddenly shouted something in Italian to Giuseppe. She seemed agitated, and I asked her what had happened.

"They murdered a small boy. Those fucking settlers! Crazy bastards! They burned him alive!"

Rafaela was not one to hide her feelings about any topic, in particular one that lay close to her heart, such as the Occupation. She was talking about the case of Mohamed Abu Khdeir, details of which would come out during the days and weeks that followed.

Abu Khdeir was a sixteen-year-old Palestinian from East Jerusalem who was kidnapped and murdered by three right-wing Jewish settlers, ostensibly in revenge for the murder of the three Israeli teenagers who had been abducted and executed shortly thereafter. During a part of his trial the following November, months after I returned to the US, the ring leader of the three settlers, twenty-nine-year-old Yusuf Haim Ben-David, recounted the sequence of events leading up to the murder.[12]

Although he maintained his innocence by reason of insanity, he did not dispute the facts of the murder. He stated that one of his two co-defendants, both minors, choked the victim, before he himself beat him repeatedly with a crowbar. Then the three of them poured gasoline down his throat and over his body before Ben-David set him on fire.

"We were hot and angry, and decided we'd burn something of the Arabs," he said.[13]

An autopsy later confirmed that Abu Khdeir had indeed been burned alive.[14] Ben-David also admitted that he had been behind the attempted kidnapping of seven-year-old Mousa Zaloum several days earlier, which had failed because Zaloum's mother had intervened.[15]

We did not have all the details of Mohamed's murder at this time, but rumors about the fact that he had been burned alive were rampant. There were also rumblings that he had been forced to drink gasoline, after which his attackers put a lit match down his throat, burning him alive from the inside.

The immediate Israeli reaction to the murder of Mohamed Abu Khdeir was predictable. At first the police refused to consider the possibility that this act could have been committed by Israeli settlers. Instead they played on the populace's racist sentiments by spreading rumors that Abu Khdeir had been the victim of an honor killing perpetrated by his father, who murdered his son because of his sexual orientation.[16] The murder sparked a series of clashes both in East Jerusalem and in other cities. Stones were thrown, and the police responded with sound bombs and rubber bullets.[17] [18]

"'After Mohamed, everything just exploded,' said his cousin Amsam Abu Khdeir. Following her relative's murder, Shufat, once a quiet leafy Palestinian suburb of Jerusalem, descended into constant chaos. Palestinians demonstrated around the clock for nearly a week over the police's ineptitude and crackdown. Border authorities also stationed themselves outside of the family home, firing tear gas into the mourners' tent."[19]

The experiences of the Abu Khdeir family constituted yet another instance of the unequal treatment by the Israeli authorities of Jews and Arabs, even those who are Israeli citizens. The homes of the families of the suspects in the murder of the Israeli teenagers were demolished without trial and immediately after the discovery of the bodies. The Abu Khdeir family, on the other hand, called for weeks for the destruction of the homes of the defendants in their son's case, but their pleas were ignored even after the guilt of the suspects had been established with little doubt.

"Everyone knows that they [the defendants] are monsters and they are killers. They murdered my cousin in cold blood," said Amsam."[20]

Mohamed's murder was condemned by many Israeli politicians, but their sympathies were rejected by the Abu Khdeir family, who blamed the government for stirring up anti-Arab sentiments in Israel, which they claimed played a pivotal role in their son's murder.[21]

"'We demand that the Israeli government find the criminals, and protect the Palestinian population,' said Ishaq Abu Khdeir, Mohamed's uncle. 'Everyone in the government is responsible for this crime, from [Prime Minister Benjamin] Netanyahu down.'"[22]

16
Thursday, July 3
Everybody is Affected

I WAS THE ONLY PASSENGER. The driver, Nabil, was thirty-two years old, and he had been driving a *service* for fifteen years. He did not mince words when I asked him about the Occupation.

"The Israelis are not human," he said. "They are animals. They just take and take and take. Even after they have stolen everything, they will just find something else and then take that too." I noticed there were pictures of four young children—two boys and two girls—hanging from his rear view mirror.

"They are very cute," I said to him, using the Arabic word *zareef*, which can be translated as "pleasant" or "having a good sense of humor." This was the word closest to "cute" that I knew, and I was relieved when he appeared to understand my meaning, beaming at me.

"They are everything to me," he said. "I want them to have a better life than me, but I am not very hopeful." Then Nabil told me about his brother, Iskandar.

"He was picking olives from our trees when he was ten years old. This was fourteen years ago. He stepped on a mine, and he lost both of his arms and legs. An aid organization in Ramallah paid for him to go to America, to San Francisco, where he stayed for years. He had many, many surgeries and lots of physical therapy. But he still cannot work. And he is very depressed because of his situation. All he wants to do now is marry. But what woman will marry a man with no arms and legs?"

It was amazing to me how all-pervasive the Occupation seemed to be. How many random people had I met, who had had their lives irrevocably, some tragically, altered by it? The previous time I had taken a taxi, the driver, Aziz, told me the police had fined him 40,000 shekels and kept him under house arrest for one-and-a-half years, depriving him of his livelihood. I remembered Marwan, the man I had talked to while waiting for the body of the mentally handicapped man murdered by the army in al-Ain refugee camp to arrive at the hospital in Nablus. Marwan had shown me his deformed hands, which had been broken by soldiers during the First Intifada and which made it difficult for him to find work. Now there was this driver and his brother Iskandar. Everyone in Palestine, it seemed, had his own story of suffering at the hands of the Occupation.

I already knew the answer to the question before I asked it, but I wanted to have confirmation.

"Did the Israelis pay for what happened to your brother? Did they even apologize?" Nabil simply laughed a mirthless laugh and grimly stared at the road ahead of us.

**

My phone rang. It was Abdullah. He was talking so quickly that it was almost impossible to understand him.

"Slow down, Abdullah. I can't understand you. What happened?" I asked, my voice getting louder with alarm.

"No, James. It's good news. My brother is being released next week! I'm so happy! I have not seen him in three years! My brother is coming home! We are going to have a huge party! You are all invited!"

**

In the *service* from Ramallah to Nablus I thought about the demonstration at Kufr Qaddum that we were supposed to attend the next day. Rafaela and Giuseppe had indicated they did not want to participate, and Abdullah said he did not want to go for fear of being arrested so close to the release date of his brother.

"I have waited so long for this. Wouldn't it be awful," he said to me, "if I was arrested just a week before my brother was released? I don't want to take any chances."

So it would be just me and Selim, two relative newcomers, going to Kufr Qaddum the following day. It felt like I had lived a whole lifetime since I had last attended a demonstration, although I knew it had only been two weeks.

Kufr Qaddum has a long history of conflict with both settlers and the occupying force.[1][2][3] It is a village with a population of 4,000 inhabitants, located just off the road connecting Nablus to the city of Qalqilya.

There are several illegal settlements near Kufr Qaddum, some of which have been built on village lands, including Kedumim. In 2003 this settlement was expanded beyond the road to Nablus which caused the government to forbid Palestinians from using it. A trip from Kufr Qaddum to Nablus, which in the past had taken fifteen minutes, now necessitated a voyage of forty minutes along a bypass road. The closure of the road was more than a mere inconvenience for the residents of the village; it destroyed its connection to Nablus, the economic center of the region. The decision resulted in the descent of Kufr Qaddum into high unemployment, abject poverty, and despair. In 2011, perhaps emboldened by similar actions in the villages of Ni'lin, Nabi Saleh and Bil'in, the villagers of Kufr Qaddum began protesting against the closure of the road to Nablus.

17
Friday, July 4
Protest at Kufr Qaddum

Over a breakfast of Korean noodle soup the next morning, Selim and I discussed some of the details of how we should behave at the demonstration. We were both novices when it came to these protests, and I felt it was important to go through some of the obstacles we might encounter.

"If either one of us gets physically involved with the soldiers, the other has to join him. It will be much harder for them to arrest both of us," I reminded him. This was standard ISM procedure that we had been taught during training.

Ever since I had come close to being struck by a teargas canister at a protest two weeks earlier, I had been thinking about how lucky I had been to avoid being hurt.

"We should always stay together, Selim." Again standard ISM procedure mandated that ISMers stay in pairs at demonstrations.

"But I want more. I think only one of us should be taking pictures or videos at the same time, while the other one is watching for teargas. When you're looking through your lens, it can be hard to see the teargas that might be coming from a different direction."

I knew there was not much we could do about getting shot. If the army wanted to shoot us, they would. It was as simple as that. We agreed that we would use any nearby buildings as cover as much as possible if the soldiers began shooting. My experience at Ni'lin had taught me that a seemingly innocuous situation could turn dangerous in a matter of seconds, and I reminded Selim to be careful.

I checked my equipment one last time before we left. I had a camera with a memory card and a charged battery; phone with credit and a charged battery to communicate with Selim in case we were separated and had to call Tali, an Israeli ISMer, if I was arrested; running shoes in case we had to run from the soldiers; long pants out of respect for the villagers and to minimize the damage done by flying teargas canisters; a *keffiyeh* to protect myself from teargas and the prying lenses of the soldiers' cameras. I was ready.

Selim and I walked to the *Duwar* to catch the taxi, arranged by Abdullah, that would take us to Kufr Qaddum. After twenty minutes or so our driver, a man in his twenties, warned us.

"There's a checkpoint coming up. If they stop us, tell them you're going to Tel Aviv. There's a border crossing near Qalqilya."

I wondered if we were posing a significant danger to the driver. What would happen to him if the soldiers found our *keffiyehs* or my cell phone filled with Palestinian contacts? The worst that could happen to Selim and me was arrest and a few days in prison possibly followed by deportation. But what about the driver?

I thought about Aziz, who had been apprehended taking illegal workers to the border with Israel and fined 40,000 shekels, in addition to being placed under house arrest for one-and-a-half years. I suppose he could always claim that he did not know we were activists. Hopefully the soldiers would believe him.

We were lucky and passed through the checkpoint without being stopped. A few minutes later we turned off the main road and drove up a winding road through the village of Kufr Qaddum. We were dropped off next to a mosque in front of a small general store, which to my surprise was open given that it was Friday and Ramadan.

We were early. It was eleven o'clock, and the demonstration would not start for at least two hours, so Selim and I decided to investigate our surroundings. I knew that the demonstration would begin at the mosque and then proceed along the road to the edge of the village, a distance of some 200 meters.

We walked along the protest route, which was entirely empty save for a few kids kicking around a soccer ball. We passed the last house in Kufr Qaddum and were presented with a startling scene. The paved, light-colored road continued straight out of the village, but as soon we passed the last house we were walking on a dirt road that was remarkably black in color. There were several large boulders and many smaller rocks and stones lying on it, giving it a menacing appearance that was in stark contrast to the pristine white of the buildings in the settlement, which lay just a few hundred meters in the distance.

It was difficult to look straight along the road and not have the settlement enter your field of vision. It was that close. It seemed like you could just walk along the black road and end up in the white settlement, but I knew this was impossible. Rising from the road to the left was a hill that was mostly bare or rock-strewn and had only a few trees. To the right of the road was a large abandoned brick building and a hill that sloped down, away from the road.

I assumed this was the settlement of Kedumim, the expansion of which was responsible for the closure of the road from Kufr Qaddum to Nablus and which was the subject of the ire of the village's inhabitants. In all of the other demonstrations that I had attended at Bil'in, Nabi Saleh and Ni'lin, the settlements were some distance from the villages, but that was not the case here. I wondered what it was like to live so close to the people who had done you so much wrong and be forced to literally look up at them every day.

After a while the village began to stir. A young man, sporting a *keffiyeh* that covered his face, drove a tractor pulling a trailer filled with tires, and he dropped them in the middle of the road, a few meters past the abandoned building. Others, with their faces covered, carried the tires from where they had been dropped farther up the road, where the boulders made it impossible for the tractor to go. They threw the tires onto one big pile, and one of the older men lit them on fire. The flames quickly grew, and soon there was a roaring fire which produced thick black smoke that rose in the sky.

"The wind usually blows in the direction of the settlement," one of the men explained to me. "It lets them know we are here and that we are not going to go away."

The day was hot, and standing near the fire was becoming unbearable. There were maybe a dozen young boys sitting in among the trees on the slope of the hill to the left. Selim and I found an unoccupied tree and sat down, leaning against the trunk. I felt relieved to be sitting in the shade. Within a few minutes we were joined by six of the boys who appeared to range in age from four to ten. I knew that international activists on occasion attended the demonstrations at Kufr Qaddum, and I was surprised that we, as foreigners, still attracted the attention of the children. Perhaps it was Selim. Asians were not a common sight anywhere in Palestine.

I asked the children whether they were fasting. Most of them nodded solemnly, and only the youngest, shyly clasping his older brother's leg, said he was not. Asking kids about fasting was usually a good conversation starter, like talking about Ronaldo and Messi.

After a few minutes the children got bored and started throwing small stones at a nearby tree. An older boy, who was lying on the ground with his eyes closed, was suddenly set upon by two of the younger ones, and a playful wrestling match ensued. As I watched the boys, I thought about the bond that must exist between them. Starting at a very young age, they came here every week to protest not just against the closure of the road to Nablus, but against their poverty, against their fathers being unemployed, against their cousins being in prison, against their electricity being cut, against their uncle being killed: in short, against the Occupation. Sometimes they would be teargassed, arrested or shot at, but they would come back every week. I knew that if any one of them were ever hit by a bullet, all the others would risk their lives to carry him to safety. The circumstances thrust them all into an early and painful adulthood. That they would go through all these experiences together must create an almost unbreakable connection between them.

I joined Selim who had wandered off to the abandoned building by the side of the blackened road.

"Look, James. There are the soldiers," he shouted. There were probably twenty or thirty of them, and they were standing at the top of the hill to our left. I felt exposed, standing in the middle of the road, but none of the villagers around me seemed to give them a second thought, so I pulled my *keffiyeh* over my face and waited. One of the little boys standing next to me on the road laughed.

"Don't worry, it hasn't even started yet," he shouted. He was right. The soldiers were just standing around. Some were lounging in the jeep that had appeared at the top of the hill on the left. A big Israeli flag was fluttering in the breeze next to it. Nothing much was happening. It was still early.

By now there were at least a hundred and fifty people on the road. I was amazed at the sheer number of small children. There must have been at least fifty, some of whom were carrying black gas masks that seemed so big for them that they could crawl entirely inside. I did not notice it at the time, but I realized later that there were no women protesters, save for a single female Israeli activist.

I saw two Palestinian journalists, whom I could identify by their blue helmets and their blue bullet-proof vests. They were sporting white tags that had been sewn onto their vests and had PRESS written on them in big blue letters. I envied the security that I assumed their credentials, and especially their vests, offered them. (I found out later that this assumption was entirely false, as a Palestinian journalist was shot in the leg with live ammunition at a demonstration in this very village late in 2014.[1])

One of the men had a megaphone, and he started haranguing the soldiers on the hill.

"Why are you doing this? Go back to your families! Leave us alone!" he shouted at them.

The first tire fire had gone out, and several of the young men carried more tires from the rear, throwing them on the ground, creating another pile in the middle of the road. Again one of the men set it on fire.

The fire was bright orange and hot, and it blocked much of the view of what was happening behind it. Suddenly, I saw the outline of a bulldozer approaching the burning pile. It was at least twice as tall as a person and just as wide, an enormous monstrosity that was threatening to devour all of the tires and possibly any protester that was unlucky enough to get in its way. At first only the shovel was visible, the thick black smoke obscuring the rest of it, but after a few seconds I could see the four bright headlights which hinted at the bulldozer's immensity. Eventually the bulldozer emerged in its entirety, and I could see that it was driven by a single soldier protected by a cage.

As the driver started to push the pile to the side, some of the braver protesters, maybe ten of them, some wearing gas masks and others with only their *keffiyehs* to protect them, ran up and started throwing rocks at the bulldozer. The ones who approached closely, to within a distance of a few meters, managed to score direct hits, but the rocks bounced off the protective cage harmlessly. It must have seemed like flies attacking a grizzly bear, and I was not sure whether the driver even noticed as he continued to clear the pile.

For a second I felt a little sorry for him, all alone and surrounded by people who wished him harm. On occasion, when the bulldozer seemed clear of the pile, and the stone throwers got too close, it turned as if to pursue the protesters. They would run desperately to get away, at which point the bulldozer would return to its mission of clearing away the debris.

One of the protesters close to the bulldozer was carrying a big Palestinian flag, and when the bulldozer turned to pursue him, he merely stood there defiantly, reminding me of that iconic photo of the unarmed protester in Tiananmen Square standing alone in front of a tank. The moment was lost when the bulldozer came too close, and the man ran for his life.

Protesters face off against bulldozer at Kufr Qaddum.

At first the smoke obscured them, but after a short while I could discern three or four jeeps on the road behind the bulldozer. Some of the young men had climbed a few meters up the hill and were using their slingshots to hurl small stones at the jeeps and the soldiers that were inside them. It looked like the soldiers were wearing helmets and protective armor and were carrying shields and weapons, and it seemed again that there was no way the youths with their slingshots would be able to harm them. I did not think that dissuaded the young men.

I knew the protest was not about inflicting damage on the army. It was about letting everybody know that the villagers were not going to go away. I laughed at the people who called Palestinians violent because they threw stones at these protests. Throwing stones at heavily protected soldiers armed with machine guns and firing teargas did not constitute violent action in my opinion. It was all about context. If a six-foot-four man weighing 200 pounds attacks a much smaller woman, and she tries to fend him off by punching him in the stomach, would you say she is being violent?

At this point the soldiers in the jeeps unleashed a barrage of teargas. While the handheld weapons could only shoot one canister at a time, the guns mounted on the jeeps were capable of firing much more frequently, at least a few per second, it seemed to me. At the same time the soldiers at the top of the hill joined in and started shooting teargas as well, and by now the canisters were streaking across the sky from all directions, the white gas trailing behind them and contrasting beautifully with the deep blue of the sky. Some of the gas was being fired from a jeep that was hidden behind the still burning pile of tires, and it looked like it was emerging directly from the thick column of black smoke. Perhaps the monster was not the bulldozer, but the smoke itself, spitting out teargas at the protesters who had dared come so close.

The teargas was deceptive in its beauty. It was dangerous, potentially deadly even. Some of the protesters were undeterred by the barrage of teargas, but everybody else ran. Some of the canisters behaved unpredictably after they hit the ground, bouncing to and fro, as if kicked by an unruly child, but in reality propelled by the hissing gas that was still escaping from them. Sometimes a protester would stop one of the canisters, pick it up and hurl it back at the soldiers while it was still spewing out its contents, which would usually elicit a huge cheer among the throngs of demonstrators.

The gas was now everywhere, in the sky and spreading on the ground, and I did not know in which direction to run. It seemed that the important thing was merely to run, to get away from the danger. The direction was almost irrelevant. And I did not care so much about the gas itself as being hit in the

Teargas at Kufr Qaddum.

head by a canister. Then, as suddenly as it had begun, it was over. There was no more gas in the sky, and what there was just above the ground was dissipating slowly. People around me, even some children, were hunched over, coughing, while their friends held them and talked to them in comforting tones. Some of the older boys, those that had been closest to the jeeps and had inhaled the greatest quantity of gas, were coughing the most violently, tears running down their faces.

Eventually the ranks of the Palestinians thinned considerably, and it seemed that the demonstration was finally winding down. The protesters were exhausted, not simply because of the teargas and the stress of facing off against the soldiers, but mostly because of the fasting.

"The demonstrations don't last as long during Ramadan," an old man told me. "You need to drink water to fight the Israelis."

The Israeli soldiers were probably bored by now anyway. I noticed that the ones at the top of the hill started creeping closer to the village, which was behind us, but nobody seemed to pay them any mind. Perhaps there was no nefarious purpose to their movements. Maybe they just wanted to go home. The old man confirmed my thoughts.

"It's over," he said to me.

I called the man who had taken us from Nablus to Kufr Qaddum that morning, and he agreed to pick us up a couple of hours later. Selim and I walked back to the convenience store next to the mosque in the village and waited. We were both parched, and the streets were empty by now, and I decided it would be permissible to drink something. I bought a Coke and downed it in a few seconds. It felt wonderful.

As we sat on the stone steps in front of the store I looked at Selim. His face was streaked with a combination of sweat and dirt, and his glasses were so smudged that I wondered how he was able to see out of them. His hair was standing on end, and his clothes bore remnants of the soot from the burned out road.

"Haha, Selim!" I said to him. "Look at you! Now you are a real activist!"

I thought about what would happen if we were stopped at the checkpoint on the road back to Nablus. It must have been clear from our appearance that we were not tourists. There was not much we could do about this state of affairs, so I did not give it any further thought. However, I did breathe a sigh of relief when we passed by the checkpoint and I noticed that there were no soldiers manning it.

***

In the evening I found out about the beating of Tariq Abu Khdeir. Tariq was the fifteen-year-old cousin of Mohamed Abu Khdeir, the teen who had been burned alive and beaten to death by Jewish extremists in East Jerusalem earlier in the week. Mohamed's murder had triggered a wave of protests in the family's neighborhood over the following days, and Tariq, a bystander at a protest that took place on Wednesday, was apprehended by two Israeli policemen and badly beaten.

There were two aspects, other than his relationship to his cousin, of Tariq's situation that caused it to garner more attention than the usual beatings

PROTEST AT KUFR QADDUM 111

administered by the police normally receive. First, it had been captured on video, and its brutality thus became clear to everyone. Equally important was the fact that Tariq happened to be an American citizen.

Tariq's bruised and swollen face was everywhere on the web, and it was difficult for me not to cringe every time I looked at it. Both of his eyes were blackened, and his mouth was grotesquely disfigured.

"I could not believe it when I saw him. His face was totally distorted. It was going off to the side. It was really hard for me," said his mother when she was allowed to visit him at the hospital.[2]

The video, widely available on the internet, was even more difficult to watch. It showed two Israeli border guards, dressed in black, holding down Tariq's body in what appeared to be a yard filled with rubbish. The bigger of the two proceeded to punch Tariq before stomping on and then administering several kicks to his head. He then punched Tariq in the head a few more times for good measure and followed this up by pounding on the back of Tariq's now motionless body with his heavy boots. His comrade joined him in carrying Tariq out of the yard, the victim's head now lolling forward. The first border guard then kicked his head in brutal fashion one more time. At this point a third man joined the first two to aid them in carrying Tariq's body.

The part of the beating captured on video lasted less than two minutes, but this was more than enough to horrify me. Probably the most difficult part to watch was the last kick administered by the soldier. It was particularly vicious, and there was no need for it as Tariq was clearly unconscious by this time, his head hanging forward from his body like a useless appendage. There could be no justification for it other than the soldier's rage, hatred, and obvious contempt. It reminded me of the "blue bra girl" video from Cairo, and it stirred up some of the same emotions in me. It was hard to watch human beings behaving in this manner.

I could not imagine the pain that the Abu Khdeir family was going through in the aftermath of Mohamed's murder. To be confronted with the brutal and very public beating of another member of the family must be unimaginable.

Tariq later woke up in the prison of al-Muskobiya, and he found that he had been shackled and blindfolded. He was interrogated about his role in the protest at which he had been detained. The police alleged that he had been with a group of youths armed with knives and throwing Molotov cocktails, but Tariq said he was merely an innocent bystander.[3] An eyewitness later corroborated his version of the events.[4]

The US State Department exerted pressure on the Israeli authorities, and they released Tariq from prison after three days.[5] He was placed under house arrest for nine days, but he was never formally charged.[6]

The Israeli government was not finished with the Abu Khdeir family, as the authorities arrested yet another cousin at the end of July, causing the US government to accuse the Israelis of singling out the relatives of Mohamed Abu Khdeir.[7]

I had talked to enough Palestinians to know that beatings at the hands of Israeli soldiers were commonplace, but it was altogether different to see this practice in action. The viciousness of the attack I saw in the video made it all seem much more real to me. I knew that Tariq had been saved from a fate much worse because of his citizenship and because the event had created such a publicity storm. What happened to those kids who were not as fortunate to be citizens of Israel's most important benefactor or whose abuse was not documented on film? They would slip by the world's awareness like so much of the abuse and injustices heaped upon the Palestinians. The thought reminded me of why I was there: to be another set of eyes and ears to bear witness to the oppression under which they lived.

18
Saturday, July 5
Beaten by Settlers

Selim left Nablus, and I would not see him again before he departed Palestine. I was sad to see him go. Of all the international ISMers, he was probably the one I had connected with the most. Although I had known him for less than three weeks, we had experienced a wide range of emotions together including fear, which had created a strong bond between us. I hoped I would see him again at some point in the future.

***

Abdullah and I were in Rafidia hospital. It was here that I had waited for the body of Ahmed Khaled, the mentally handicapped man who had been murdered by the Israeli army, and the memories of that day came flooding back to me. It had been my first day in Nablus, and it was hard to believe that it had been only three weeks earlier.

In the reception Abdullah asked for the whereabouts of the victim of the previous night's settler attack, and we were shown to a room on the third floor. Lying in one of the beds was a young man in his early twenties who was sporting a cast on his right leg. At first glance this appeared to be his only injury, but when I looked at his face I realized that he had been hurt in a more important and fundamental way. His expression showed that he was still deathly afraid and that the fear had made him almost catatonic. It was an expression I had never seen before, and it frightened me. He was somewhat conscious, but it was clear to me that he was in no condition to talk. His father, who was sitting in a chair next to him, waved us away, insisting that we come back the following day.

***

Later that same day I found out what had happened to Tareq Adeli, the young man in the hospital. According to a report by *Ma'an News*,[1] Adeli, who was from the village of Osarin just south of Nablus, had been approached by a group of settlers in his home village at around midnight the previous evening.

The settlers sprayed gasoline on him and pulled him into one of their vehicles before taking him to a field and attacking his legs with a hatchet. They then left him bleeding in the field before Adeli managed to call his father, who eventually took him to the hospital in Nablus.

I could only imagine what the young Palestinian must have gone through. At the moment when the settlers dragged him into their car, he must have feared that his fate would be the same as the one that had befallen Mohamed Abu Khdeir just days earlier.

19
Wednesday, July 9
Tear Down this Wall

THE ISRAELI ARMY HAD STEPPED UP ITS AIRSTRIKE CAMPAIGN in Gaza the day before, hitting 435 targets, killing twenty-three Palestinians and wounding 122 others.[1] I had been expecting this since the discovery of the bodies of the three teenaged settlers, but it was nevertheless a shock to realize it was actually happening now.

***

On June 12, the day that three teenaged Israeli settlers were kidnapped, Prime Minister Benjamin Netanyahu declared that he had proof that Hamas was behind the kidnappings. Shortly thereafter the Israeli army launched Operation Brother's Keeper, one of whose goals was the destruction of Hamas' operations capabilities in the West Bank.[2] During this campaign ten Palestinians would eventually be killed and over one hundred arrested,[3] including many former prisoners who had been freed in the 2011 Gilad Shalit prisoner exchange.[4] Among those arrested were almost all of Hamas' leadership in the West Bank.[5]

Hamas reacted to the IDF campaign by firing rockets into Israel, to which the Israeli air force responded with air strikes on targets in Gaza. According to reports, between June 12 and July 5, sixty-two rockets were fired into Israel while eighty air strikes were launched into Gaza during that time.[6] On July 4 Hamas offered to cease its rocket attacks if Israel agreed to stop its air strikes, while Israel threatened to engage in major offensive if the rockets did not stop.[7] The next day Hamas offered a truce on the condition that Israel lift its import restrictions on Gaza and allow the PA to pay Hamas' civil servants, which it had been neglecting to do.[8]

I doubted that these attempts at preventing the escalation of violence were genuine, but they failed in any case. Over the following few days, there were both rocket attacks and air strikes,[9] until Israel finally began its military campaign in earnest on July 8.

***

In the afternoon Rafaela invited Olaf and me to join her in an action organized by a group of Palestinian activists.

Olaf, the former coordinator of the Hebron team, was staying in Nablus because his visa had expired, and he decided it would be safer for him here. In Hebron ISMers had to show their passports almost on a daily basis because of the ubiquitous checkpoints in the city, and it would be likely for one of the soldiers to notice the expired visa. He feared he would then be deported and possibly even banned from ever entering Israel again. The chances of getting caught in Nablus would be much smaller. Eventually, he would have to explain the visa at the airport, but at least that would be in Israel, not in the Palestinian territories.

Today was July 9, and it was the ten-year anniversary of the ruling of the International Court of Justice, which stated that the Apartheid Wall violated international law. The group of activists wanted to make a statement against the Wall, and its leaders had decided on a two-pronged approach. Some of them would use hammers to punch a hole through the Wall, while others would attempt to scale it. They would go to Qalqilya, the city closest to Nablus from which the Wall could be reached.

Both climbing the Wall and chipping away at it would be largely symbolic gestures. The previous summer I had visited a section of the Wall near Abu Dees, which was next to Jerusalem. Months earlier some young Palestinians had hammered away at the Wall, not expecting much to happen. They had accidentally hit a weak spot and a big section had crumbled, leaving a hole almost large enough for a car to drive through. You could still see the results of the effort the Israelis had made to repair the damage. Perhaps the activists were hoping something similar would happen at Qalqilya.

We walked to the *Duwar* and climbed into a rickety bus that the activists had procured to take us to Qalqilya. There were roughly thirty people, and the mood was jovial. The leader was a Palestinian man in his fifties. He was telling jokes to the entire bus throughout the ride, and every few minutes everybody would erupt with laughter.

I was somewhat surprised by the lack of seriousness with which these activists were treating the current situation, which in my estimation was quite dangerous. I doubted that the Israeli authorities would look too kindly on a group of Palestinian activists who were trying to destroy a part of the Wall, and I knew this was not the only danger. There were checkpoints all over the West Bank, and I remembered that there was one on the road to Qalqilya, which I had taken to the demonstration at Kufr Qaddum the previous week.

What if the bus were stopped and searched? Most likely all of the Palestinians would be arrested and the foreigners deported.

There was a commotion in the back of the bus. The activists had arranged for six enormous hammers to be brought to the Wall so they could attempt to punch holes through it. Now it was discovered that only a single hammer was on board. There was a short debate on whether to try to find more hammers or to continue with just the one. Because of time constraints, they decided on the latter. This action was not getting off to a good start.

The activists had chosen Qalqilya as the location for the action against the Wall because it was conveniently positioned close to Nablus, but also because the Wall had caused residents of Qalqilya a considerable amount of suffering.

Qalqilya is a town surrounded on three sides by the Wall, which makes reaching the city extremely difficult. It means that travelers can only enter along a single road, and even this road has a checkpoint that the Israelis can close whenever they want. A villager living a few kilometers to the south of Qalqilya is now forced to travel much farther to go to the market to buy the food he needs.

The effect on the city's economy has been predictably disastrous. Because Qalqilya no longer attracts shoppers from nearby villages, prices have dropped precipitously, and farmers have a much more difficult time eking out a living. A resident told me it was possible to buy ten kilograms of tomatoes for the equivalent of $3, while that would cost you many times more everywhere else in the West Bank.

In Qalqilya some farmers must use a gate manned by Israeli soldiers to reach their fields. One such gate is Hableh gate. The gate is open twice a day for half an hour: once in the morning and then again in the afternoon. If a farmer happens to be late in the morning or the Israeli soldiers are in a bad mood, the farmer will not be allowed to work that day. During harvest time, this has particularly serious consequences, as it implies that his crops will rot in the field. If a farmer is late returning home, and he finds the gate closed, he will be forced to spend the night in the fields.

I had visited the city in the summer of 2013 with a guide, Abu Hassan. He had spent several years in Israeli prisons, and he told me that his brother had been shot by a settler when he was thirteen.

Abu Hassan said that the Israelis have decreed that only the rightful owner of the farm may pass through the gate. The owner, in most cases an old man, is therefore prohibited from hiring others to help him work the fields. This policy has the dual effect of making the farm much less productive than it would otherwise be, as well as removing opportunities for work from young men in the village. The effect on the local economy is devastating.

The bus pulled into Qalqilya after another twenty minutes, and we stopped outside a small house where we were to pick up the ladder we would use to climb the Wall. A young man came running towards us. He had lent the ladder to a friend who needed it to paint his house, but if we were willing to wait half an hour, he could get it back for us. The situation was becoming quite comical. Here we were, thirty activists, sitting in a sweltering bus, waiting for a man to finish painting his house so we could use this ladder to protest the Israeli occupation. We had in our possession a single hammer with which we would hopefully make a dent in the Apartheid Wall.

Forty-five minutes later the man returned with a rickety ladder that looked like it would break in a strong wind. Even worse, it was at most three meters in length. What was going on here? I knew the Wall at Qalqilya was much higher than three meters. How were we supposed to climb it with this tiny ladder? This was fast becoming ridiculous. Nevertheless, we loaded it onto the bus and set off for the Wall.

We parked, and as we walked the hundred or so meters from the bus to the Wall, the futility of our enterprise became increasingly evident. The Wall here was huge—at least six meters high—with another meter of metal fencing on top. The ladder was completely useless here, and I wondered why two of the younger Palestinians in our group were bothering to carry it. The Wall appeared to be a massive, concrete monolith that could withstand the pounding of thousands of hammers, to say nothing of the solitary one in our possession.

As we approached closer I saw that there was a great deal of graffiti on the bottom section of the Wall, although not nearly as much as in other towns such as Bethlehem or Qalandiya, both of which sport beautiful work by artists such as the famous Banksy.

We passed by a portrait of Che Guevara, and somebody had spray-painted *Gaza, Free Palestine* and *Our Pen is Mightier Than Your Sword* nearby. I also noticed the name of Mohamed Abu Khdeir, the Palestinian teenager who had been burned alive by extremist settlers in the wake of the discovery of the bodies of the three abducted Israeli teens.

There were two observation towers that rose slightly above the top of the Wall. They were solid concrete, and the windows at the top were too small for us to discern whether there were any soldiers inside. Olaf, who had a powerful zoom on his camera, told us he could not see inside the windows either. Two of the people in our group threw stones at them, and when nothing happened we decided that the army was most likely not nearby.

By this point the others had also realized that they would not be able to scale the Wall with the ladder, so they put it down. Instead, they picked up the hammer and began swinging it at the giant concrete structure in front of us. It was heavier than the young men had anticipated, and each man would take three swings before passing it on. After a few minutes they had made no discernible impact and decided to give up. I felt bad for them since they had had high hopes for making a statement that would at least cause the Israelis to respond. Instead, it was unlikely they had even made them notice.

After a short discussion some of the activists decided to walk back to the bus to retrieve a few old tires. If they were unable to attract the attention of the Israelis by climbing the Wall or punching a hole through it, perhaps they could do so by lighting a fire near it. Three or four of the activists threw the tires onto the ground by the base of one of the observation towers and lit the pile on fire. The fire caught quickly, and after a few minutes we could see a column of thick black smoke that, because of the prevailing wind conditions, was unfortunately blowing back towards Qalqilya. As the noxious smoke drifted eastward, I thought it was more than a little ironic that the people most affected by our protest seemed to be the local residents.

Protesters burn tires at the Apartheid Wall in Qalqilya.

By this time, we had not yet seen a single Israeli, but I assumed the army would eventually notice the smoke and come to investigate. It was probably a good time to leave.

Suddenly, I heard loud yelling and noticed a middle-aged man dressed in a gray *galabeyya* running towards us. He was the owner of the land next to the part of the Wall near the observation tower, and he was incensed.

"What are you doing?" he yelled at one of the activists. "Why are you setting those tires on fire? Don't you know that the Israelis are going to come? And what about you? You're going to be gone by then. And who do you think they're going to blame for this mess? My son has already been to prison once. Are you going to help me with the farming when he's sent to prison again?"

The man was furious, and justifiably so, I thought. Had the activists not even considered the effects their actions would have on the local population? One of the activists had told me on the bus that their organization always went to painstaking efforts to ensure that the locals supported their actions, but clearly that had not been the case here. Perhaps there had been some discussion with a local popular committee, but certainly nobody had consulted the farmer.

***

Later that evening I had a conversation with Rafaela about what had happened. I felt strongly that the behavior of the activists had been inappropriate, that they should have taken into account the effects of their actions on the locals. They should have asked the farmer whether he supported what they were going to do, because he was the one most directly affected by it. Maybe he was not willing to make the sacrifice of having his son end up in prison. In any case it should be his decision, not that of the activists. Rafaela, on the other hand, believed that the Occupation affected everybody and that all Palestinians had to be willing to pay the cost necessary to resist the Israelis.

20
Friday, July 11
Live Ammunition at Kufr Qaddum

I WAS GLAD OLAF WAS IN NABLUS and would be joining us at the protest at Kufr Qaddum. He had spent the previous summer working for ISM, and I thought his experience would be useful for both me and Giuseppe, especially the latter, since this was to be his first demonstration in Palestine.

I called the driver who had taken me to Kufr Qaddum the previous week, and we met him at the usual spot at the Duwar. We were lucky again this week, because the checkpoint on the road from Nablus to Qalqilya was unmanned, and we arrived without problems in the village.

The day was, as usual, extremely hot, and we rested on the shaded patio in front of the village convenience store. There were six young boys sitting with us, joking around. I asked them if they were fasting. One of them, apparently the oldest, pointed to each of the boys in turn and told me whether he was fasting or not. The boys nodded proudly as they were pointed out. Only the very youngest, who looked like he was five years old, was not fasting.

"Why are you not fasting?" I asked him.

"I'm too young," he said simply.

I recognized a tall blond man whom I had seen at Kufr Qaddum the previous week. He wore his long hair in a ponytail, and he was dressed in a t-shirt and shorts, the only activist in the village to be so attired. I assumed he was European, but he introduced himself to me as an Israeli.

"We should not be treating the Palestinians in this way. They are human beings, not animals," he said to me when I asked him why he was here. "The Occupation has to end. It is bad for the Palestinians, and it is bad for Israel. How can a country consider itself to be advanced, when it treats people in this way?"

I often wondered why I had not seen more Israelis at these demonstrations. I knew there were several who attended the weekly protests at Nabi Saleh on a regular basis, but I had not noticed any here at Kufr Qaddum. The risks for them were much lower than they were for the foreigners, not to mention the Palestinians. Of course they could be shot or injured just like the rest of us, but their situation would be radically different if they were arrested. Tali, the ISMer whom we were supposed to call if we ever found ourselves in Israeli custody, told me that an Israeli would spend at most one day in prison before being released, while foreign activists faced longer prison time and possible deportation. The Palestinians, of course, would have to deal with circumstances that were of a different category altogether.

Where then, were the Israeli activists? Would they be ostracized by their friends? Were the societal pressures they faced that prevented them from acting on behalf of the Palestinians so overwhelming? I knew that the answer was "yes." It was illegal for them to attend demonstrations or even set foot in parts of the West Bank, and there were legal repercussions for various other forms of standing in solidarity with the Palestinians. For example, the "Law for Prevention of Damage to the State of Israel Through Boycott," passed by the Knesset in 2011, makes the support of the boycott of Israel, such as through the Boycott, Divestment, and Sanctions movement, illegal and a supporter subject to a prison sentence. I knew of many Israeli pro-Palestinian NGO's, and I admired the members of Breaking the Silence,[1] a group of former IDF soldiers who spoke out against the Occupation, often revealing the shameful acts they had been forced to perpetrate against the Palestinians.

I was expecting—and hoping—despite the difficulties they faced, to see larger numbers of Israelis at the weekly demonstrations. Even though acting against the Occupation was difficult, did Israelis not care about doing what was right? There are books that deal with the prevalence of extreme racism and prejudice in Israeli society, which has shifted to the right in recent years, but I was sure there were many Israelis who felt differently.

One of the reasons I felt so strongly about the Occupation was that my taxes were playing a large part towards furthering it. To put it simply, as an American taxpayer, I felt complicit.

But it was not just because I was American. It was also because I considered the Occupation to be merely another example of Western colonialism, and it was my people—Westerners—who were perpetrating it. It seemed to me that Israelis should have similar feelings of responsibility. After all, they were the ones who voted for the government that was committing these crimes. They should be the ones acting to prevent these horrible events from occurring.

Abdullah felt even more strongly about this issue, going so far as to say that he would have nothing to do with Israelis whatsoever.

"They were the ones," he said to me once, "who were living in the homes stolen by the Israelis from my grandparents. I appreciate the Israelis who protest against the Occupation, but that is not enough. They have to leave." Abdullah wanted all the Israelis to leave Palestine.

"They stole the land from us, and we should get it back. Not just Gaza and the West Bank. All of Palestine. It belongs to us. They came and took it. That is not right."

"What about the Israelis who were born here? It is their home, too, isn't it? They've never lived anywhere else. Do you expect them to uproot their lives and move someplace they don't know anything about?"

"Well, it is the same as what happened during the *Nakba*. Almost a million Palestinians were kicked off their land. The same thing should happen to the Jews now. If we kick the Jews out, at least we're not kicking them off their own land. We're forcing them to leave *our* land. That is a big difference."

"But they weren't the ones who took your land. It was their grandparents. Should they be forced to suffer for the crimes their grandparents committed? Should white Americans be punished for what their ancestors did to the native Americans or for slavery? Do you believe that Germans today should be held responsible for the atrocities of the Nazis? If we continue like this, the violence never ends."

Most Palestinians I talked to were not as extreme as Abdullah in their views. They believed Palestine should be a single country in which Israelis and Palestinians could live together in a democracy. Most agreed that some allowances could be made to account for the fact that this new nation would now be home to two distinct peoples.

By this time dozens of people had gathered in front of the store and were preparing to march down the village street that eventually turned into the soot-covered road by the demonstration site. At the head of the group of activists were about a dozen young boys, ranging in age from five to ten. They were all carrying signs protesting the Occupation and the assault on Gaza and calling for a revolution. A black-haired boy wearing a bright yellow shirt held a sign that read:

"Rocks will understand if people won't. Whenever Palestine decides to rise, it will conquer. No matter how much fire you start, we will put it out. Can't you see that we're already tanned from coping with its heat? And if you killed all the revolutionaries and the old people, the disabled, then even the stones will turn into rebels against you. Revolution!"

A small boy wearing shorts and a t-shirt carried a sign exhorting the Israelis to stop committing their crimes in Gaza. "The Zionist massacres against our children, women, and elder people are crimes against humanity. We won't be terrorized, we will keep on, united. Gaza, you are free."

Marching with the boys was a middle-aged man shouting into a bullhorn, "People of Palestine! We will have our freedom! This is for our brothers in Gaza!"

The children were followed by a group of slightly older boys, some of whom wore gas masks on their heads like baseball caps, ready to be pulled down at the first sight of the noxious gas used by the army. Others sported *keffiyehs* to cover their faces. Then there were the teenagers and young men, most of whom were also wearing gas masks or *keffiyehs* and some of whom were carrying slingshots. The rear of the procession was made up of the older men of the village, and a few journalists and foreign activists were sprinkled throughout. There were no women whatsoever.

When we reached the outskirts of the village, we saw the Israeli soldiers scattered around the hillside to the left of the blackened road. Somebody had already set the pile of tires at the end of the road ablaze, and the black smoke was drifting towards the settlement on the hill. Perhaps on this day the settlers would actually be aware of the fact that that the local population was none too happy with their presence. If the wind direction held, maybe they would even have to close their windows to avoid inhaling the fumes.

Olaf was taking pictures near the tires, and Giuseppe and I were a few meters behind him, watching as a couple of protesters placed stones in their slingshots and hurled them at the soldiers on the hill. I was not sure about their effectiveness, but the slingshots were a beauty to behold. Most of the boys using them wore *keffiyehs* over their faces. They grabbed whatever stones they could find and placed them gently in the slingshots, whereupon they would twirl them in a circular orbit above their heads, maybe four or five times, before releasing them towards the soldiers. I had seen this weapon used at every demonstration I attended, but I had rarely witnessed a stone actually hitting its intended target. I assumed that the slingshots were effective on occasion; otherwise the protesters would not be using them. The Israelis certainly claimed that they were lethal weapons and merited a forceful response.

Suddenly, I felt something pass just to the left of my head. It was difficult to pinpoint what had happened. There was a buzzing sound that lasted a fraction of a second. Then it was gone. It felt like it was very close, but it was hard to tell for sure. I looked at Giuseppe, who was standing a few meters away. "Did you feel that?" I asked him.

"Yes. What was that?" he replied.

My first thought was that it was a rubber bullet that had been fired to scare the protesters. But did rubber bullets make a buzzing sound when they passed by? I did not think so. And I had not heard the sound of a gun being fired. Perhaps the soldiers were using silencers today. Did guns that fired rubber bullets have silencers? Maybe the bullet had hit a rock or a tree and ricocheted in my direction. It seemed like a change of direction in the bullet's flight path might cause it to wobble, thereby creating a sound of vibration. I was merely guessing at this point. I wished I had paid more attention during the ISM training a month ago. Ayman had spent an hour explaining the various kinds of guns and bullets employed by the army. Could it have been a real bullet? Would the soldiers really be using live ammunition at a protest like this, where the threat of violence was almost nil?

I did not discover until later that it was a rubber bullet that passed by my head that day. At the time, my reaction to the event was quite different from what I had expected. I was surprised to notice that I was not frightened in the least, and I continued to take pictures at the protest, although I did try to stay lower. As I thought about it later in the day, I realized it was probably because it seemed so unreal to me. I could not see any danger, which somehow made me feel that it was not really there. The soldiers firing their guns were far away, and I could barely see them. Could their bullets really hurt me? Even if they had no weapons of any kind, I would have been much more afraid had they been closer.

Throughout my time in Palestine, I was much more fearful of being arrested than being shot. Being arrested meant physical confrontation and facing a real person, a person who was likely angry and wished me harm. Being shot was different. It was more clinical, and there were no emotions involved. It was cleaner, somehow.

Suddenly, there was a commotion under one of the trees on the hillside. A young man had been shot in the left knee, with a real bullet. Although rubber bullets could be dangerous and even lethal when fired from close range, their effectiveness deteriorated drastically and usually did not even break the skin when they were fired from a great distance.

So it was indeed live ammunition they were using today. The victim was a young man, about twenty years old. His friends had rolled up his pant leg to reveal the entry wound made by the bullet. There was not much blood. On the inside of the knee was the exit wound. Or was that where the bullet had entered?

In any case, the bullet was now gone, lodged in the dirt somewhere. His fellow protesters carried him to the ambulance, which was waiting just out of range of the soldiers' rifles. He grimaced as he supported himself by wrapping his arms around the necks of two of his friends, while two others gently held his legs, trying to avoid touching the wound. The ambulance sped away as soon as the young man was placed gently in the back.

I was shocked. There had been no warning: no teargas, no skunk water, no open confrontation, no buildup, just a shot without a noise of any kind. The soldiers were clearly using silencers, robbing their victims even of the millisecond between the moment when the bullet leaves the rifle and when it strikes human flesh and bone.

I was used to seeing conflict that begins innocuously and escalates slowly. Two people exchanging words, then perhaps some shoving and eventually punches thrown. This defied all conflict logic, if there is such a thing. There was no beginning. No slow crescendo that would allow one of the parties to avoid real harm. It seemed like a law of sorts had been broken.

"Those soldiers are Druze," a man standing next to me observed. "They are Arabs, and they are shooting their own brothers. They are usually the ones we have to be careful of. The Jews treat them badly, and they try to impress their masters by being as harsh to us as possible."

The protesters proceeded as if nothing unusual had happened, some of them continuing to either throw stones at the soldiers or use their slingshots with the same objective. As I watched a skinny boy load his slingshot, I wondered what he must have been thinking. Was he not afraid? He had just watched his friend get shot with live ammunition for doing what he himself was about to do. Was there any temptation on his part to simply drop his slingshot and run home? Even if the social pressure not to flee must have been enormous, he could have taken steps to protect himself without anybody noticing. He could have slowly crept further away from the front, throwing rocks with a little less frequency. But he was doing just the opposite, running closer to the soldiers, swinging his slingshot with just a little more vigor, screaming just a little louder.

Then it happened again in the same way as the first time: no warning or noise of any kind. Suddenly, a boy was on the ground, clutching his leg. Four protesters rushed to pick him up and carry him back to the ambulance. As they passed me, I could see that this time the wound was on the fleshy part of his leg, just above the knee, and that there was a great deal more blood. The victim was wearing a ski mask. When I looked into his eyes, it seemed like he was calm, but perhaps he was just in shock. I watched his friends carry him past me, towards where the ambulance should have been. But the driver had not yet returned from his first trip to the hospital, so the most recent victim would have to wait. His friends carefully placed him on the ground, in the shade, next to a house, so he could lean against its cool wall. Three of them quickly returned to the battle, while one remained to comfort him, speaking to him softly.

I began to be concerned about my own safety. I noticed that both victims had been throwing stones before they were shot, and I assumed that I would be a less likely target, because I was doing nothing other than photographing. Why would they aim at me, when I was just a bystander? But this was ascribing to the soldiers qualities that I was not sure they possessed. I knew that soldiers sometimes shot and even killed protesters who were not engaging in behavior that could in any way be construed as violent, as they had done during the protest at Ofer prison just months earlier. That incident had been captured on video and garnered international attention for a short time.

I also remembered the demonstration at Nabi Saleh the previous summer, when my friend Jessica had been shot in the arm with a rubber bullet while she was running away from the soldiers. The only weapon in her possession at the time had been a cell phone camera. The incident with Jessica reminded me that the protection afforded me by my white skin was by no means absolute. Enough Western activists had been killed or injured by the IDF.

Even if I was not a primary target for the soldiers' bullets, this did not guarantee that I would not be the victim of an accident. Perhaps that was what had happened earlier. The bullet that had whizzed by my head might have been intended for someone else. I decided to stay away from the hillside, which was where both of the protesters had been shot thus far.

And then another man was shot; I had not even seen it. This time it was in the groin. Were the soldiers slowly setting their sights higher and higher? The knee, the thigh, the groin. What was next?

I had heard that Israelis tended to aim for the groin area, when they shot at protesters. Perhaps this latest soldier was just a better shot than his comrades. Or maybe it was the same shooter all along, and he was just improving with time. Maybe he had been nervous for the first two shots, and now he was settling down, his nerves calmed by his early successes. This victim too was carried to the ambulance, which had returned by now, and he was placed inside to join the boy who had been shot in the thigh. There was a heated conversation between the driver and some of the others. I was unable to catch it all, but it seemed like the driver was itching to leave, while the others wanted him to wait in case there were other victims. The driver relented, and the ambulance waited.

And then another man was shot. Blood was pouring from his arm. He was also wearing a ski mask, and I could not see his face, but he had a sizeable belly, which made me think he was significantly older than the others. He must have been seriously hurt, because, despite being hit only in the arm, he was unable to walk and needed considerable assistance to make it to the ambulance.

And then, suddenly, it was over. The protesters slowly straggled back to the village. Maybe it was my imagination, but it seemed to me that everyone was quieter than usual. Altogether five people had been shot. I knew it was not unusual, but it was also not something that happened every day, and it must have affected the villagers. It was the first time in my life that I had witnessed someone being shot with live ammunition, and I really was not sure how to react. It felt surreal, and I found myself wondering whether it had really happened. The fact that it was also the first demonstration I had attended at which no teargas had been used made it seem even more unreal.

***

After we arrived back at the apartment in Nablus, I went up to the roof to be by myself and try to process what I had just witnessed. I felt numb, and it worried me. I knew the words *should* and *normal* had no place when it came to feelings, but it still felt to me that there should have been some reaction. I simply felt nothing. Five people who were protesting against the injustice meted out by an occupying power had been shot in cold blood. And I had seen it. Should I not have been raging against the unfairness of it all? Should I not have been moved to tears by the suffering of the victims? Was I feeling okay because it was not me who had been hurt, that I was one of the lucky ones who was safe?

There is a famous thought experiment in which a man is confronted by a general. The general has at his disposal a powerful army, to which he can give the order to have a million people in a foreign country executed. The only way to save them, the general tells him, is for the man to agree to have his left pinky finger cut off. The man does not hesitate and accepts the offer. It is just his finger, and he can save a million souls. But the night before the deed is to be done, he is terrified of facing his fate. He thinks about a tall, powerful, masked man swinging a cleaver down onto his finger, severing it from his hand, blood spurting everywhere. He can imagine the almost unbearable pain, and he begins to sweat. All night long he tosses and turns, unable to sleep.

In the second part of the experiment, the general does not offer the man a choice. He simply informs him that the following day one million people will die and that there is nothing he can do about it. How will the man react? He will feel sorry for the victims, and he will most likely be upset for a time, but eventually he will calm down and go to sleep. He will not be nearly as affected in the second scenario as he is in the first. When given the choice between the saving of a million people and his finger, he will always choose the people. But the thought of losing a finger is much more terrifying to him than the idea of a million people he does not know meeting their deaths.

The story illustrates how conflicted people can be. They are willing to make enormous sacrifices in order to do what is right, but at their core what terrifies them most is the thought that their own personal safety is at risk. Perhaps my own reaction to the shootings merely indicated that I was a normal human being, one who is primarily concerned with his own well-being.

21
Sunday, July 13
Cheering the Massacre

ABDULLAH TOLD US THE NEWS FROM GAZA. It was grim. Today was the sixth day of the attack, and thus far 167 people had been killed and over 1,000 injured.[1] It looked like things would get worse before they would improve. Tens of thousands of Israeli reservists had been called up and were massed at the border with Gaza with tanks and artillery.[2] It appeared that a ground invasion was imminent.

Abdullah also told us about a report that I still find difficult to believe.[3] A Danish reporter, Allan Sorensen, was in Sderot, an Israeli city two kilometers from the border with Gaza, when he took a picture that subsequently received a great deal of international attention. The photograph, taken at night, showed roughly twenty young people sitting in plastic chairs near the top of a hill. Most of them were wearing shorts, and they appeared to be having a good time. Sorensen wrote that they were Israelis who had come to the hilltop to watch army jets fly their missions over Gaza, and that they clapped and cheered loudly whenever a blast was heard. In the foreground was the picture of an Israeli teenager with a big grin on her face. It was clear that she was enjoying herself immensely.

In another article, more details were given.[4] The people on the hill were sitting on camping chairs and sofas, eating popcorn and smoking *sheesha*. The atmosphere was very much that of a party. The reporter described the scene moments before a bomb struck the city.

"The talk on the hill falls silent for a moment. Suddenly, the night sky lights into a powerful flash, while a high column of fire rises in Gaza. A few seconds later the earth is shaken by a dull roar. Now cheers break out on the hill, followed by solid applause."[5]

Several of the Israelis at the viewing party are quoted.

"We sit and look at Israel creating peace."

"And it's also just good fun."

"It's great to be here. You can feel the thunder and see the rockets. It is a quest for excitement."

I wished the reporter had asked them how they felt about the children being killed by those bombs they were cheering, the lives being ruined. I imagined they would have said that Hamas was to blame, that Israel was only defending itself. Still, I thought, assuming one could convince oneself that Israel's response could somehow be justified, what kind of moral gymnastics would allow one to applaud at the deaths of innocents? I supposed the people would argue that the Palestinian children would grow up to be terrorists, and that it was better to kill them now. Even if I could go so far as to imagine such a thought process, it should only lead to the realization that this task, though necessary, was grim and should be accomplished with extreme distaste. What caused the leap, then, that the Israelis performed to reach the place where they could enjoy the deaths and suffering of innocent people? Were these spectators no longer human? Or were they simply a product of a society that pounded into the heads of its citizens the idea that the whole world was out to kill them; that its supposed supporters had let them down once before and stood by idly as a maniacal dictator tried to have them all destroyed; that they could only rely on themselves to defend themselves; that anything was permissible to ensure it would never happen again?

22
Monday, July 14
Why Palestine?

Tonight we had dinner on the roof of our building. It was a warm evening, and Sofia, a young activist, cooked a sumptuous pasta dinner for us all.

Since their arrival in Nablus a few days earlier, Sofia and her three friends had leaned on Olaf, their fellow Dane, for support. He had taken great care to talk to them about life in Nablus and with ISM and to show them the ropes, but he had left the country the day before.

Though they were inexperienced, they seemed eager to learn, and I found it to be a pleasure to interact with them. They infused the apartment with a youthful energy that was refreshing. It took a few days for us to become comfortable with each other, but once we did, we would sit at the dining room table for hours discussing what we saw during our days in Nablus as well as the events in Gaza. I admired them for being brave enough to work as activists in Palestine at such a young age. Comparing them to myself in my early twenties, I was amazed by how much more mature and well grounded they were than I had been. Eve and Johan were already engaged to be married, and all four of them seemed to have been friends since childhood. They liked to joke around with Abdullah and me, and what began as serious discussions often ended with uproarious laughter.

Sofia's extensive dinner preparations seemed to have put everybody in a good mood. We finished the meal of pasta and vegetables, accompanied by the local bread prepared at the bakery that was located just down the street, owned by our downstairs neighbor. I was the only one in the group who did not smoke, but everybody else lit up a cigarette, and we leaned back against the low roof wall and relaxed. It was dark by then, and the lights of Nablus twinkled.

I often wondered what drove people, young and old, to come here to work on behalf of the Palestinians, and it was this question I now asked the group.

"Palestine is the only country in the world that is currently under military occupation," Rafaela said, "and it has to stop. The Occupation has lasted for close to fifty years. Every day Israel abuses the Palestinians. It steals their land and engages in human rights abuses, while the world stands by and watches."

"Most informed people would not argue with you, Rafaela," I countered. "There is a lot of injustice here, but that is not my question. There is injustice and suffering everywhere. Why did you choose Palestine? Horrible abuses are taking place all over Africa, for example. Why did you not go to the Congo, where millions of people have died in recent years?"

The New York Times' Thomas Friedman might argue that the reason is anti-Semitism, writing that "singling out Israel for opprobrium and international sanction—out of all proportion to any other party in the Middle East—is anti-Semitic, and not saying so is dishonest."[1] I felt that Friedman's conclusions about anti-Semitism required quite a leap of logic on his part. After all, calling any nation to account for its crimes should be considered a worthy and necessary endeavor, even if other countries are engaging in worse behavior. However, the question remained. Why Israel?

"It's the only military occupation in the world, James. Why don't you understand that?" Rafaela repeated.

"Military occupation is just one particular kind of crime one people can commit against another. There are plenty of others that are worse. Look at what is happening in Syria. Over 200,000 people have been killed, not to mention the injured and the homeless.[2] Why did you choose not to get involved in that?"

It was a question I had often asked myself. According to some sources, roughly 50,000 people had died in the Arab-Israeli conflict since 1950, a figure that includes casualties from the major wars during that time.[3] While this was surely a horrific number, it certainly did not compare to the astronomical death tolls in Syria, the Democratic Republic of the Congo, or many other places.

I knew that the Arab-Israeli conflict garnered a great deal of international attention because it was occurring in a place of interest to the adherents of the planet's three great monotheistic religions. But I was not religious, and this was certainly not an issue of concern for me.

"As a Westerner, I feel a particular responsibility for what is happening here," Johan chimed in. "It is because of Western support that Israel is allowed to commit these crimes. If the West did not turn a blind eye to what is happening here, there is no way that Israeli soldiers would be killing Palestinian children without fear of being punished. Israel can do whatever it wants, because it knows we still feel guilty about the Holocaust. I think if more people in the West knew about the human rights abuses here, they might put some pressure on their governments to be more critical of Israel." Naia agreed.

"And that is why we are here. So we can let the people back home know what we see here. It's one thing for them to read newspaper reports. It's more effective if we tell them in person what we saw."

As the only American taxpayer, I knew that I had probably contributed more to the Occupation than anybody else in our group. Since 1997, Israel has received $3.1 billion annually in aid from the United States, most of it military, and since its founding in 1948, it has received over $100 billion.[4] (In September of 2016 the Obama administration agreed to increase the aid package to Israel, committing a staggering $38 billion over the decade beginning in 2018.[5]) But American support of Israel is not limited to the financial domain. The US regularly vetoes UN resolutions that call Israel to account for its crimes. Since 1967, this has occurred forty-one times,[6] and since 2001, the United States has vetoed no fewer than ten security council resolutions pertaining to the issue of the Palestinians. (The extent of the American diplomatic commitment to Israel can be evidenced by the backlash when Obama, weeks before he left office, refused to veto UN resolution 2334, which stated that Israel's settlement activity was a "flagrant violation" of international law and demanded the cessation of all Israeli settlement activity.[7] The resolution, which is not legally binding, passed 14-0, with the US being the only member of the security council to abstain.)

Sofia, who was sipping her tea slowly, said she had come to Palestine because she believed the conflict was really about colonialism and racism.

"As Westerners, especially Europeans, we have a centuries-long history of occupying lands belonging to others. It is time that we stopped doing this. We have destroyed the peoples and cultures of an endless number of places: the Americas, Africa, Australia, the Indian subcontinent, the Far East, and the Middle East. Although this exploitation is still happening on many levels—economic and cultural—all over the world, there are few places where it is as explicit and overt as it is in Palestine." Sofia's lower lip trembled as she continued explaining her thoughts about this issue, which was obviously as emotional for her as it was for most of us.

"When it started a few hundred years ago, it was all about race. The white man thought he was better than the brown, red, and yellow 'savages' and had the right to take their land and its resources. It's not as obvious today, but it's still the same issue. The language has changed. That's the only difference. Now we talk about 'terrorists' instead of 'savages.' The underlying theme is the same. We are better than they are. So, yes. That's why I am here. Because I don't agree with this racist bullshit!"

23
Tuesday, July 15
The Gaza Onslaught Continues

Today the Israelis killed sixteen more Palestinians in Gaza, bringing the total to 194 in the eight days since the offensive began.[1] I read that the Egyptian government had attempted to broker a ceasefire between Hamas and Israel, but that it had been rejected by Hamas. Hamas continued to fire rockets into Israel, bringing the total number of rockets to 1,147, which caused the death of one Israeli citizen.

We obtained most of our news about what was happening in Gaza from the online versions of *Al Jazeera* and *Ma'an News*, as well as from our Facebook feed. ISM had a couple of activists in Gaza, but our communication with them had been sporadic at the best of times, and it was now even more difficult to stay in touch with them.

Every once in a while I checked the BBC website for an update of events, but I was disappointed by its pro-Israel bias. I had always had a relatively positive impression of BBC as presenting a mostly impartial point of view, but its coverage of the Gaza massacre changed my opinion. (As I look back on it now, I realize that I had been very naïve. My previous estimation of the BBC had more to do with the atrocious and entirely one-sided coverage of the Middle East by American news organizations, compared to which the BBC was a bastion of fairness and balance.) I was not the only one who was dismayed by the job the BBC was doing. There were demonstrations outside BBC's London office that were protesting the network's skewed coverage of the assault.[2]

The BBC website displayed a graphic that I found extremely troublesome.[3] The graph showed, for each day of the conflict, the number of rockets fired at Israel by Hamas, as well as the number of targets in Gaza hit by Israel. For a typical day, one would see the blue bar, representing the number of rockets used by Hamas, below—but not too far below—the red bar, which indicated the number of targets hit by the Israelis. By placing both bars on the same graph, the network was implying that one Hamas rocket attack was somehow roughly equivalent to one Israeli airstrike. This was an attempt to show that there was a semblance of balance in the conflict. The implication was that it was a war between two relatively equal parties, instead of an absolute massacre. The fact that a supposedly neutral news organization was trying to frame the conflict in this manner was extremely disturbing to say the least.

The notion that the Hamas rockets were equivalent to the Israeli weapons was, of course, absurd. These rockets, though certainly potentially terrifying for the Israeli civilian population, were mostly crudely constructed and nowhere near as devastating as the American made hi-tech armaments employed by the Israeli air force. In fact, throughout the attack on Gaza, though Hamas managed to fire 4,591 rockets into Israel as stated by the IDF,[4] only seven Israeli civilians were killed as a result. Meanwhile the IDF hit 5,226 targets in Gaza, and according to the UN,[5] killed at least 2,104 Palestinians, including 1,462 civilians, of whom 495 were children and 253 women.

24
Thursday, July 17
Waleed Comes Home

THE NEWS FROM GAZA TODAY was heartbreaking. Four children, who had been playing soccer on the beach, were killed by a shell fired from an Israeli naval gunboat.[1]

Somebody had taken a video of the grisly scene and posted it on YouTube. It appeared that the cameraman made the film shortly after the boys were killed and probably before the bodies were moved. He walked among the tiny bodies, which looked to be about ten meters apart, filming each of them. The boys were all lying face down in the sand, and they all had significant burns on their bodies. One of them had his legs splayed out at unnatural angles, making for a particularly disturbing image.

As I watched the video, a familiar feeling of rage began to rise in my chest. What had these boys done? The Israelis had killed them like they were worthless, and the world did not care. There would most likely not even be an apology for these four young, innocent lives snuffed out and for the countless others ruined. Yes, there would be some outrage in the international community, but in the end, what would change? The US would still send its weapons, and Israel would continue its rampage. Netanyahu would get on TV and blame Hamas for everything. But what was Hamas supposed to do? Sit by and watch as Israel continued to impose its brutal blockade on the population of Gaza?

***

Netanyahu placed the blame for the current trouble in Gaza squarely on the shoulders of Hamas. After all, they were the ones who fired rockets at innocent civilians in Israel. It was Hamas who, in its charter, declared that it could not accept the existence of Israel. (Scholar Noam Chomsky claims that Hamas long ago renounced this charter,[2] and others argue that Hamas does offer de-facto recognition of Israel, since it was willing to enter a unity government with the PA, an action that implies acceptance of all previous PA-Israel agreements. In his diatribes against Hamas, Netanyahu conveniently neglected to mention that the platform of his ruling Likud party itself includes the statement: "The Government of Israel flatly rejects the establishment of a Palestinian Arab state west of the Jordan river." This is of course at odds with the acceptance of the right of self-determination of the Palestinian people.[3])

Israel was the home of the Jews, victims of the Holocaust, one of the greatest atrocities in the often bloody history of mankind. Now Hamas wanted to cast them from their biblical home and force them into a harsh world and possibly yet another Holocaust. If there was anything the Jews learned from that tragedy, it was that they had to be self-sufficient and could not rely on the protection of anyone else. They had to stand up against Hamas. Their very existence depended upon it.

This was the Israeli narrative, and it was the version that the mainstream media fed to the masses in the West. It was the truth, but it was not the entire truth and, like many political narratives, was taken entirely out of context.

All of the events in Gaza had to be viewed in the larger context of the Israeli occupation of Palestine, in particular the almost decade-long siege of Gaza, which has kept the inhabitants in a constant state of misery. Was Hamas, which did not have the access to modern weapons that Israel did, not entitled to defend itself against this action? According to international law, it certainly was.

The Israelis might argue that it perpetrated the siege in reaction to the terrorist activities of Hamas, making it a defensive action rather than an offensive one. But then one must go a step further back and ask about the justifiability of Hamas' violence prior to this latest siege. This cycle of blame ends only when one arrives at the root cause of the entire dispute, which is the establishment of the state of Israel in 1948. Simply put, the Zionists had no right to be there, despite what the Balfour Declaration of 1917 indicated. They were given land that belonged to others, and everything that has happened since then is a consequence of this action.

Does this mean that the Jews of Israel have no right to be there now? Of course not. Several generations of Jews have now been born and raised in Israel, and it is their home, and they should be allowed to stay. But should they be allowed to subjugate the native population and keep them in a state of poverty and misery? Again, the clear answer is no.

I once asked Abdullah how he felt about Hamas.

"Usually I do not support Hamas. I don't like how strict they are about religion. But I am so proud of them right now. They are the only ones who are resisting. Look at the PA. They are just collaborators and traitors. You know how you can tell that the Israeli army is about to enter Nablus? When the PA disappears. You see no police on the streets. The army orders them to leave, and they just go, like dogs. You can say what you want about the violence of Hamas. But at least they don't just give up."

***

My phone buzzed. It was Abdullah. He was shouting.

"He's coming home, James! Can you believe it? Waleed is being released today! After three-and-a-half long years!"

"That's fantastic, Abdullah! I'm so happy for you and your family!"

"I want you guys to be there when he comes. All of you. My parents are going to pick him up at Ofer prison around dinner time, and then they're all coming home together. We'll have a huge party at my house. And I want you to be there when he arrives."

I looked at Waleed's poster, which was hanging on the wall of the dining room in the Nablus apartment. He was wearing a tight black t-shirt and jeans, and he was kneeling in front of a red background. Although he was arrested when he was eighteen, he looked like a boy in the photo. Waleed was in the middle of the picture, and he was surrounded by head shots of three prominent members of the Popular Front for the Liberation of Palestine (PFLP), including George Habash, its founder, and Ahmad Sa'adat, the general secretary, who was currently serving a long prison sentence. At the top were written the words "Popular Front for the Liberation of Palestine." Just underneath was a message expressing solidarity with Waleed, saying that neither jails nor jailors could scare him, because he had the support of his comrades.

I arrived at Abdullah's village in the early evening with the four Danish ISMers. As we walked down the narrow streets leading to his house, I noticed dozens of red PFLP flags flying from the roofs of the nearby buildings. The closer we got to his house, the greater the concentration of flags. As we turned the final corner, I saw an enormous banner that had been hung between the roof of Abdullah's house and that of the house across the street. The banner bore Waleed's image, as well as those of the same PFLP secretaries whose pictures I had seen on the poster in our apartment. (Tragically, it was the presence of these flags at the party that the Israeli authorities used to haul Waleed back to prison almost two years later in March of 2016. The flags proved, claimed the army, that Waleed was still an active member of the PFLP, which constituted a crime.[4])

Festooned to the wall on the building opposite Abdullah's front door was a green, red, black, and white Palestinian flag that dwarfed the banner flying above. Waleed's release was clearly a momentous event in Awerta, one that the entire community would take part in.

Abdullah greeted us with enthusiasm, but I could tell that he was also nervous with anticipation. To work off some of his nervous energy, he suggested that we go for a walk.

Awerta was small, and after a few minutes we were walking along a narrow dirt road that led out of the village and into the surrounding hills. The sun was just about to set, and the heat of the day had dissipated. It was still light enough for me to see the trees and the light-colored houses that dotted the hillsides.

Abdullah was pensive.

"James, I've been waiting for this moment for so long, and now it's almost here. I am happy, but I'm also numb. I don't know how to feel. I'm afraid that when he comes back, he will be a stranger. Who knows what he went through in prison? I did not see him once the entire time he was there. Even my parents were only allowed to visit him a few times. What will he be like? Will he remember how to smile and laugh? He was just a boy when he went away, and now he is a man. But not just an ordinary man. A man who was in an Israeli prison and who was probably beaten regularly." I did not know what to say, so I remained silent. Abdullah looked at his watch and continued.

"Right now he's having dinner with my mother and father. They picked him up at Ofer an hour ago, and they will be arriving in Awerta in another hour." I clapped him on the shoulder.

"It's going to be ok, Abdullah. It will be just as it was before he went away. You two are brothers. That is never going to change."

Several times Abdullah had complained to me about Waleed's absence. Waleed was the oldest male child, and his responsibilities had been taken on by Abdullah after his brother was imprisoned. He had been forced to play a greater role in the family, which included looking after his younger sisters. I knew that he looked forward to Waleed's return, when he would not only once again enjoy his brother's companionship but also resume living his somewhat more carefree life.

A crowd had gathered back at Abdullah's house in anticipation of Waleed's arrival. I was astounded at the sheer number of people. I would estimate that there were roughly a hundred men and boys in the street next to his house. People were hugging, laughing, and crying, and the mood was festive. Abdullah's face was shining. Everybody was waiting for the star to arrive.

"Let's go, everybody!" Abdullah shouted at us. The Danish ISMers and I, as well as some of Abdullah's relatives, piled into a van, so we could drive to the entrance of Awerta, where we would greet Waleed and his parents. Five or six cars accompanied us through the streets of the village until we reached the intersection with the main road.

It was dark, but I could see Waleed sharing an embrace with several young men. He was older than he had looked on our poster, but it was clearly him. His head was almost completely shaved, and he looked more muscular. These were his buddies, and they had arrived a minute or so ahead of us. Waleed's aunt, Abdullah's father's sister, jumped out of our van after we had stopped and ran towards him, crying. Waleed hugged her briefly before turning back to his friends.

I noticed that there seemed to be a hierarchy at work here. Waleed's friends were at the top, followed by his family. Even Abdullah was only greeted with a kiss on the cheek and a few words. Perhaps the real reunion with the family would take place at the house, after the party had died down. But I felt bad for Abdullah and especially for the female relatives, who were prevented by local custom from attending the street party that was about to begin. They would have to wait to fully welcome Waleed back from prison.

The convoy of cars that led back to Abdullah's house was significantly longer than the one that had gone out to meet Waleed, and it was also much louder. The occupants of the cars were joined by local villagers who were either leaning out of the windows of their houses or simply lining the streets on this joyous occasion. People were waving flags, screaming, and crying, taking pictures and playing music. Fireworks were set off in celebration. Boys climbed onto the roofs of the cars and waved at the onlookers below.

I found it extremely touching that seemingly the entire village of Awerta had turned out to welcome back one of its sons. The mood was one of relief that Waleed had made it back in one piece, but there was also a sense of victory, of which the Palestinians had precious few. It seemed that Waleed had vanquished the occupiers simply by returning to his village alive. They had tried to destroy him, but they had failed because he was too strong, and here he was, a hero, even stronger than before he had been taken away.

The party did not begin in earnest until the convoy of cars arrived in front of Abdullah's house. By this time the crowd, which consisted of males of all ages, from five to ninety, had swelled to several hundred. The women, of which there were roughly thirty, had crowded onto the roof of the house and were watching the proceedings from above. The only women on the street were the ISMers, foreigners being excluded from the patriarchal traditions.

Getting out of one of the cars, Waleed, who was wearing jeans, a white t-shirt, and bore the traditional red-and-white *keffiyeh* on his shoulders, proceeded to greet seemingly every male resident of Awerta. Each greeting consisted of four kisses on the cheek followed by a hug, a process that lasted maybe ten seconds. Waleed was surrounded by dozens of well-wishers, and he often disappeared from view, but, being taller than almost everyone involved in the celebration, I was able to catch sight of him from time to time. I thought he looked tired, but he soldiered on, satisfying the desire of everybody who wanted to greet him. When he encountered a particularly close friend and smiled, I saw Abdullah in that smile. It made me sad to know that my good friend had been without his big brother for the last three years. Those three years were gone, snatched by the Occupation not just from Waleed but from Abdullah and his entire family. It seemed a cliché to say it, but Waleed had gone to prison a boy, and he had emerged a man, and his family had missed the transformation.

I was amazed by the sense of community I was witnessing. It seemed that all of Awerta had converged on Abdullah's house. Everybody wanted to be a part of this reunion: from the very young to the old and infirm. I was touched when every once in a while Waleed would bend down to greet a young boy, offering him the same four kisses and hug that he provided to the adults.

Waleed's father, a fit-looking man in his fifties with close-cropped grey hair, seemed happier than his son, and he did not stop smiling the entire evening as he accepted well-wishes from his friends, relatives, and neighbors.

After half an hour somebody handed Waleed a microphone, and he gave a short speech. The acoustics were bad, and I had difficulty understanding him, but it seemed that most of his talk centered on the recent events in Gaza. Israel was engaging in criminal and immoral activity, and the entire world, most especially the United States, was just looking on.

***

We returned to Nablus at around midnight. Before I went to bed, I checked the news to see what had happened in Gaza during the day. The headline on the Israeli website *Ynet News* read "IDF sends ground troops into Gaza, calls up 18,000 reservists."[5] An IDF spokesman was quoted in the article.

"We are now entering the second part of the operation. We delivered a hard blow to Hamas. We attacked thousands of targets, destroyed infrastructure, hurt operatives. Large [numbers of] ground troops are taking over targets in the Gaza Strip, operating against tunnels and infrastructure."

The official neglected to mention another consequence of its attacks on Gaza: the by now 200 Palestinians, most of them civilians, that had perished in the bombings.[6]

25
Saturday, July 19
Five Sons Lost to the Occupation

The United Nations Works and Relief Agency (UNWRA) defines a Palestinian refugee as "a person whose normal place of residence was Palestine during the period 1 June 1946 to 15 May 1948, and who lost both home and means of livelihood as a result of the 1948 conflict."[1]

UNWRA also defines the descendants of male refugees to be refugees themselves. The number of Palestinian refugees has grown significantly since 1950, when the organization first began administering the refugee camps, from 750,000 to roughly 5,000,000.

The camps, of which there are fifty-eight in Jordan, Lebanon, Syria, the Gaza Strip, and the West Bank, are defined as "a plot of land placed at the disposal of UNWRA by the host government to accommodate Palestinian refugees and set up facilities to cater to their needs," and they currently host approximately one third of all of the refugees.[2]

The term *refugee camp* implies a notion of temporariness, and there was at first an assumption that the inhabitants would soon be resettled to their homes. In fact, UN General Assembly Resolution 194, adopted on December 11, 1948, called for the refugees to be allowed to return to their homes on the condition that they be willing to live at peace with their neighbors. Israel, however, rejected this interpretation of the resolution and has refused to allow the return of the refugees.

Over the years, as the inhabitants of the camps came to grips with the fact that they would not be allowed home, they replaced the tents with more permanent, concrete shelters, which have become their homes in some cases for close to eighty years.

Living conditions in the camps vary a great deal depending on their country of location, but as a general rule they tend to be poor and "have degenerated into wretched inner-city ghettoes."[3]

In the summer of 2015 I spent a month living in the Palestinian refugee camp of Shatila, located on the outskirts of Beirut, and I later wrote about the horrifying conditions:

The camp, originally built for 4,000 residents, is contained in an area that is in the shape of a square of side length less than one kilometer. With the recent influx of refugees from the war in Syria, the current population is estimated to be close to 25,000. This high concentration of people makes itself felt in the ubiquitous crowds that fill the narrow alleyways, in the piles of garbage that accumulate too quickly for the trash removal workers to keep up with, in the many buildings that extend skyward to accommodate the residents, and in the lack of open spaces in the camp. Living conditions are horrifying. Electricity is cut for at least twelve hours a day, and the tap water is so salty that it corrodes the faucets. Guns are present throughout the camp, and tensions, already high because of the extreme overcrowdedness, often explode to the point of physical conflict.[4]

Writing about the Balata camp on the outskirts of Nablus, *The Economist* in 2013 stated that its "alleyways are caked in filth, . . . almost half the working-age adults have no jobs, and the UN's once-prized classrooms are as overcrowded as the rooms where the families live. Children sometimes leave school unable to write their names."[5]

***

Abdullah picked us up in the morning, and we drove in a *service* to the gate of the Old Askar refugee camp in Nablus, where we were met by a young man named Moneim. He remembered me from a meeting several weeks earlier, and he shook my hand warmly, as if we were long lost friends who had not since each other in years.

"Welcome to Old Askar," he said to us proudly, and he led us to a women's center, which was not far from the gate.

A smiling woman in her fifties opened the door of the center after Moneim knocked. She gave us a short tour of the facility, and then invited us for tea as she explained some of the work performed at the center.

"The center is primarily for the women of the camp, as well as their children. Many women have lost husbands who have died or now languish in Israeli prisons. Some are here because their husbands simply left them, and they have nowhere else to go. The main goal is to teach these women how to take care of themselves and their children. We show them how to cook, sew, and embroider. We even have a store that sells the products they make. We want them to be independent economically, so they don't have to rely on others for charity." She paused and took a deep breath.

"Some of the women have been abused by their husbands. It is part of Palestinian culture that if there are problems within the family, they stay in the family. This is a very difficult tradition to fight against. We want to show these women that they don't have to put up with this kind of violence. It is bad enough that we have to endure suffering because of the Israelis. We shouldn't have to take it from our husbands as well." She gestured towards the women in our group, and continued.

"I think it would be wonderful if some of the female members of ISM could come here to volunteer, just to talk to some of our women sometimes. It would really help them to meet such independent and confident young women.

"But please forgive me. I have been talking too much. You probably want to see some other parts of the camp." Turning towards Moneim she said, "Maybe they would like to meet Noorhan Haghighat. You should take them to her house."

As Moneim led us through the labyrinthine alleyways of the camp, I had difficulty imagining the life of the residents here. On the one hand, it seemed almost normal. There were kids kicking around a soccer ball on the street, and around the corner I saw two girls sitting on the ground eating potato chips. They waved at us cheerfully as we walked by. If you did not look closely, you would not think this was a scene from a refugee camp. But this was an illusion. This was not a refugee camp of the type I had seen on television in an area where a natural disaster has just occurred, where the inhabitants are living in tents and lining up to receive bags of rice from UN trucks. But it was still a refugee camp.

All of the houses here were crammed next to each other, with almost no space between them. They were separated not by streets but by narrow alleys, and you had to make an effort not to look into a kitchen or living room as you walked past a house.

When you look down onto Nablus from one of the nearby mountaintops, it becomes obvious where the refugee camps are. The buildings seem to lie on top of each other, and the concentration of black water tanks is much greater than it is elsewhere. You get a sense of the misery of living in a refugee camp from miles above it just as easily as when you are inside it.

The first thing I noticed about the apartment of Noorhan Haghighat was that the walls of the living room were adorned with pictures of her sons. There must have been dozens of them, and some of the portraits were much larger than life-size.

Her black hijab surrounded a face that seemed like it had decades of suffering imprinted upon it. Noorhan began crying almost as soon as she began telling her story. The sobbing made it almost impossible for me to understand her, and Abdullah translated for us.

She had had six sons, and they had all been taken from her by the Occupation in one way or another. Two were killed in the First Intifada and two more in the Second Intifada. Of her two remaining sons, one was in an Israeli prison, where he was serving a life sentence, while the other had been released after a stint there.

After every couple of sentences Noorhan's sobbing grew louder and louder. She would place both hands on her cheeks and open her mouth wide to allow the screams to escape. The crying was not like any I had ever witnessed. It was filled with anguish and pain, and it reminded me of the scenes of the carnage during Israel's assaults on Gaza that I had seen on television. One would often see footage of women wailing over the lifeless bodies of their children, and one could almost feel their pain. Noorhan's screams had the same effect on me now. But there was an important difference. Her sons had died years ago, and yet the pain seemed to not have diminished.

I found myself thinking about her future. No matter how much this woman suffers, there is no relief. Her suffering would just go on and on until, I imagined, she died. It reminded me of my own mother and how she would react if she lost even one of her children. The thought brought a lump to my throat. As I looked around me, I noticed that I was not the only one.

Olivia, a Danish woman who had joined ISM in Nablus days earlier, was crying loudly, and Sofia's face was wet with tears. Everyone was affected by the sight of this poor woman. Even Abdullah, whose life was filled with scenes of sadness and despair, seemed depressed.

We were interrupted by the woman's remaining son, Usman, who came in from the kitchen to serve us tea. He looked like an ordinary teenager, dressed in jeans and a button-down shirt, but his face had a complete absence of expression. I looked at him as he leaned forward to hold the tray of teacups close to me, and I tried to imagine what he was thinking, but his face betrayed no emotion whatsoever. Maybe the only way this boy could cope with the suffering inflicted on him in his short life was to withdraw from the world.

"He never says anything," Noorhan said, as if she was reading my thoughts. "He never goes anywhere or smiles. The house used to be full of life. Everybody was happy and laughing, and there was always something going on. Now it is completely dead. Everybody is gone. Even Usman is gone."

Noorhan sank back in exhaustion after making this declaration. She began to sob once more, her cries filling the apartment with desperation. Abdullah said that we had stayed long enough, and we filed out slowly, the women in our group shaking Noorhan's hand or hugging her. I knew many women in Palestine did not like men from outside the family to touch them in any way, so I simply mumbled *Allah yerhamhom* to her. May God bless them. What else was there to say?

***

International reaction against Israel's offensive outside the Arab world had been muted, but today at least one country made a statement. Ecuador, protesting against the massacres in Gaza, recalled its ambassador from Tel Aviv.[6] In fact, several Latin American governments would later follow suit and go even further in expelling the Israeli ambassador from their countries.

The reaction in the United States was entirely different, as on Thursday, July 17, the Senate voted 100-0 in favor of supporting the ongoing invasion of Gaza. During the debate "no mention was made of the hundreds of Palestinian civilians, most of whom are women and children that have been killed by Israel in the past ten days."[7]

100-0. I was ashamed to be a human being.

26
Sunday, July 20
Massacre in Shejaiya

IT WAS ONE OF THE BLOODIEST DAYS of the entire Gaza onslaught, although we did not find out about the events of the day until later. Most of the information below is taken from reports in *The Guardian*,[1] *The Nation*,[2] and Max Blumenthal's book.[3] The Israelis attacked the neighborhood of Shejaiya, one of the poorest districts of Gaza.

The previous day there had been skirmishes in Shejaiya between fighters from various armed Palestinian factions and the IDF, with as many as fourteen Israelis losing their lives and at least another fifty-six injured. Finding that the Hamas fighters were putting up greater resistance than anticipated, the Israelis turned to the Dahiya doctrine, the strategy named after a 2006 all-out assault on the Dahiya neighborhood of Beirut, that called for large-scale attacks on civilian populations with the goal of putting pressure on the armed forces they supported.

With this doctrine in mind, the IDF decided on a soft target: the civilians of Shejaiya. The army launched a massive artillery barrage on the neighborhood in two days, "obliterating Shejaiya in the course of about forty-eight hours."[4] A senior US military officer, commenting on the scale of the attack, told a journalist that "the only possible reason for doing that is to kill a lot of people in as short a period of time as possible."[5]

During the assault over 120 Palestinians, including many women and children, were killed.[6] Almost 300 Palestinians were injured. The attack, which began in the evening of the previous day, consisted of barrages of artillery and tank fire, which some residents said appeared to be fired indiscriminately.

There was so much firing and so much debris in the streets that ambulances had difficulty reaching the victims and, even when they did manage to get close, they sometimes came under fire themselves. At least one medic was killed when his ambulance was hit. People had to wait hours for help, and for some this was too late, as they bled to death in their apartments. The scene was horrific. There were dead bodies in the streets. The roaring of jets and the buzzing of drones accompanied the explosions of missiles and tank and artillery shells. Palestinians leaving the scene described it as a massacre. I wondered if any of the one hundred senators who had voted to support this onslaught had misgivings as they read reports of the events of this day.

By ten o'clock in the morning of July 21, the remaining residents began to flee, worsening an already critical refugee problem. UNRWA said that 140,000 refugees sought shelter in its facilities. Churches, mosques, and hospitals were being overwhelmed. Many of those fleeing Shejaiya went to Shifa, a nearby hospital.

Dr. Mads Gilbert, a Norwegian doctor, who had been in Gaza during Operation Cast Lead in 2008/2009 and Pillar of Defense in 2012, said that "those of us who worked in Shifa can say that last night was the worst night of our lives."[7]

"Israeli impunity," he continued, "is a huge medical problem. Every single dead child and adult, and all the injuries, all the amputations, are one hundred percent preventable. Cynically planned and brutally executed by the government of Israel."[8]

Residents of Shejaiya said that two days earlier the IDF had sent them messages, warning them to flee. An IDF spokesman said that many people had wanted to leave but did not because Hamas had forced them to stay, in effect using them as human shields, but this claim was disputed by international observers and reporters.

Israel and Hamas regularly accuse each other of using civilians as human shields. Earlier in the conflict, the UN had discovered Hamas arms caches in two of its schools,[9] while the IDF convicted two soldiers of using Palestinian children during Operation Cast Lead in 2008/2009 to inspect bags they thought might be booby-trapped.[10] Journalists and human rights organizations claim that Israel has used Palestinians as human shields on many occasions.[11] (I would find evidence of this phenomenon just a few days later in the West Bank village of Azzun.)

Israel regularly justifies its attacks on hospitals, mosques, homes, and schools by claiming that Hamas uses these sites for military purposes. Several times during the past two weeks the IDF produced maps claiming to prove that there were weapons stored near civilian areas. Although these claims were usually disputed by the UN, human rights groups or directors of hospitals, clinics or schools, Abdullah had a different take altogether.

"Where is Hamas supposed to store its weapons? Gaza is one of the most crowded places on Earth. There isn't any place that isn't close to a civilian building!" he said to me once.

While it is contrary to the Geneva Conventions to use civilians as human shields, it would not relieve Israel of its obligations to take care to harm the civilian population as little as possible, even if Hamas were guilty of this crime. Indeed, the Geneva Conventions state that "any violation of these prohibitions shall not release the parties to the conflict from their legal obligations with respect to the civilian population and civilians, including the obligation to take the precautionary measures."[12]

27
Monday, July 21
The Man in the Green Shirt

THE STREETS OF NABLUS WERE DESERTED. Most of the shops were barricaded shut.

As I passed my favorite falafel shop a few meters from the *Duwar*, I wondered whether this had anything to do with the violent demonstrations that had taken place here the previous night. The shop had been closed for all of Ramadan, and I missed both the tasty falafel and the exchanges I had with the owner, which usually consisted of him making fun of Egyptian politics. I had told him about my two years in Egypt, and he never failed to make a comment about the two most recent Egyptian presidents. There was a well-known YouTube video in which an old Egyptian woman wearing a green hijab cried, "Shut up your mouth, Obama! Shut up your mouth, Obama! Sisi yes! Sisi yes! Morsi no! Morsi no!" The video had made its way around the world, and the shopkeeper would, reversing the sentiment of the woman in the video, harangue me with shouts of Morsi yes! Sisi no! This was his way of indicating his support for the Muslim Brotherhood leader as opposed to the current Egyptian president, who was an army general. I asked an old man standing on the corner of the street, and he told me that all of Nablus was on strike in support of the people of Gaza.

***

In the evening, a video[1] of a particularly chilling incident that had occurred during the previous day, July 20, in Shejaiya was posted on the ISM website.

It showed the killing, presumably by Israeli snipers, of a man in a green shirt looking for his family in the rubble.

In the video there were several people, identified by ISM as volunteers and Gaza municipal workers, walking through the debris-filled streets. It turned out later that this was in the early afternoon during a two-hour ceasefire.[2] They appeared to be looking for survivors of the recent Israeli onslaught on the neighborhood.

The results of the bombing campaign were ubiquitous and shocking. Everywhere you looked there was rubble. Black smoke filled the sky in the distance, and it also billowed out of the ruins of a nearby house. How terrifying it must have been to be there during the attacks. The group walked past a destroyed ambulance, and a voice explained that all the people inside it had been killed. A group of young men passed by, carrying an injured Palestinian on a stretcher.

The man in the green shirt, later identified as twenty-three-year-old Salem Khalil Salem Shammaly, was among them. He appeared healthy and strong, but he would be dead in a matter of minutes. Some of the people close to the cameraman were wearing reflective yellow clothing. I knew this was supposed to identify them as non-combatants, and I had seen them on occasion at the protests I attended. At one of these demonstrations, at Nabi Saleh, I saw a soldier threaten a young man wearing one of these vests, and I have heard that the Israeli army routinely treats yellow-clad individuals the way they do everybody else: as the enemy.

Somebody cried out. "Is there anybody there?" It was unclear whether that person was asking for help, or whether he was offering it. The group arrived at a place where the rubble was several layers deep, and the only way to pass was to climb over it.

Suddenly, a shot was heard, and the scene became chaotic as the camera shook, presumably because the cameraman was running. It was clear that the situation had become dangerous, and the volunteers were confused. Should they run away? Should they hide? A young woman wearing a black hijab explained that she was very frightened. Something big was moving slowly nearby. You could clearly hear somebody say *dabaaba*. It is the Arabic word for tank.

The camera panned to the young woman. She held up her hands, palms open and together, as if to splash water on her face. It is the motion used by Muslims during *dua*, their informal communication with God, mainly to ask for His guidance during times of hardship or crisis. It was clear she was afraid.

But it was too late. Another shot rang out, and we next saw the green-shirted Salem lying on the ground. He had been hit, apparently in the hand.

"Can you move?" somebody asked him. But Salem did not seem to hear him.

"There is no god but God," somebody cried out. The camera was a few meters away from Salem, and there were three other men, also wearing yellow vests, twenty or so meters beyond him. But these meters may as well have been kilometers. Salem was alone, exposed, and his friends could not get to him, because they would likely be shot as well.

Salem tried to get up, but there was another shot. You could hear somebody cry, panic evident in the voice.

Ashadu ina la allah illa Allah. I bear witness to the fact that there is no god but God.

This is the *shuhada*, and believing in it is one of the five pillars of Islam. It is uttered in of each of the five daily prayers, and it is recited in circumstances surrounding death, and, in particular, during the moments preceding one's own death. You could not hear Salem recite the *shuhada*, but you could see him raise the index finger of his right hand, a motion that accompanies the *shuhada*. He knew he was going to die. Then only his left hand was moving. And then there was another shot. Salem appeared to be dead.

Salem's identity was not known when the video was posted on ISM's website, and he became simply "the man in the green shirt."

His family, who had been frantically searching for him, was able to identify him in the video the next day. Salem's father told journalist Max Blumenthal, "It's impossible to put into words how difficult it was. We waited for two or three days not knowing and when we found out, it was too difficult to handle. I have had to call on God and he helped me."[3]

A UN commission of inquiry concluded that the Israeli killing of Salem was illegal because "a civilian was targeted in violation of the principle of distinction. The fact that [Salem] was shot twice while lying injured on the ground is indicative of an intent to kill a protected person (either owing to his civilian status or to the fact that he was hors de combat) and constitutes an act of willful killing."[4]

Salem's father told the *Electronic Intifada* two years later that he wanted to see his son's murderers in court.

"Israel committed many crimes," he said, "not one: they killed Salem during a ceasefire. He was unarmed and helping others. They shot him, and then shot him again when he was helpless on the ground. Soldiers did not allow medics to take him to the hospital, he was left to bleed and his body was left out in the open for stray dogs and rodents to feast on."[5]

28
Wednesday, July 23
Human Shields in Azzun

ISM's MAIN CONTACT IN THE VILLAGE OF AZZUN is an older man named Ali, who owns a small shop just off the main circle in the town. Ali had called us earlier in the morning with the news that the Israelis had entered the village the previous night, so we had all, together with Abdullah, made the trek to investigate.

"The Israelis always come into the village to arrest people. But last night was different. They actually used locals as human shields. I've seen them do that before, too, but it seems like things are getting worse these days," Ali told us.

Azzun lies just off Road 55, the main artery between Nablus and Qalqilya. The village's main gate, which connects it to Road 55, is sometimes blocked off by the Israeli military, which places concrete blocks in the road or simply locks the gate. This forces the town's residents, as well as the residents of several nearby villages, to take long detours if they want to travel to Qalqilya or Nablus. During rush hour, especially, the alternate roads are jammed, and travel times increase dramatically. The Israeli action naturally leads to serious disruptions to the lives of many villagers, such as students who attend college in Nablus, or merchants who sell their wares in Qalqilya.

The times and duration of the closing of the gate to Azzun appear to be random, and the locals are not notified. Sometimes the gate is closed for days at a time. The army says that it blocks the road due to stone throwing in the area. As stated in a B'Tselem report[1] about Azzun, this action amounts to collective punishment and is illegal under Article 33 of the Fourth Geneva Conventions, to which Israel is a signatory. It is unlawful to punish an individual for crimes he has not personally committed. As Ali told us, the army will do more than merely block the entrance, often invading the village at night and making mass arrests. They also fire sound bombs, teargas, rubber bullets, and even live ammunition on occasion.

"As they do in the rest of the West Bank, the Israeli soldiers like to arrest children," Ali said as he rifled through some papers in his desk drawers. After a minute he seemed to have found the piece of paper he was looking for and read from it.

"There are currently sixty children from our village in Israeli prisons. Every time a child is arrested, I notify several children's organizations. But there is only so much they can do. Just last week they arrested a twelve-year-old boy. They said he had been throwing stones. They interrogated him for several hours before releasing him. Now he is with his family again, but they say he is not the same. He spends all his time inside and refuses to speak to anyone. Everybody knows about the children that are injured or killed. Their pain is obvious. But what about all the kids who are arrested, interrogated or beaten? Some of their injuries are in their hearts, and they will never heal."

Ali sighed. Clearly, he had decided to take on some of the suffering of his people, as if that would lessen their pain.

"I can arrange for you to meet some local families, so they can tell you about their experiences. But let me first tell you about what happened last night.

"On most evenings, several Israeli jeeps are stationed just outside the main gate, the one that leads to the road to Nablus. At ten o'clock last night, about fifteen soldiers entered the main square of the village. A few young men responded by throwing stones at the jeeps from a distance of approximately 200 meters. The soldiers spent the next few minutes stopping cars on the road and forcing the drivers to arrange their cars in a circle in the main square. They then made them surrender their keys. The occupants of the cars, which included women and children, were very frightened, but the soldiers did not allow them to leave. The soldiers positioned themselves inside the circle formed by the cars and began to fire teargas at the protesters, kneeling behind the occupants of the cars as they did so in order to protect themselves."

I knew that the soldiers who had used these civilians as human shields would never be called to account for their actions. The best I could hope for was that I could publicize what they had done and continued to do on a regular basis. I could write about it for ISM, and maybe, just maybe, the Israelis would realize that this negative publicity could have an impact on them. Even if this made them tone down their violence only minimally, I would still consider it a small step towards what I hoped would eventually be a just system.

***

Magdi was arrested in January of 2014. He was sixteen at the time and in his last year at school.

We were sitting in the living room with Magdi's parents and two younger brothers. I could tell that, even though the arrest had taken place seven months earlier, the family was still coming to grips with the loss of the eldest son.

"He was so full of life, always laughing. He was a comedian," his mother, a woman wearing a yellow hijab, told us, a tear in her eye. "This is our first Ramadan without him, and it makes us so sad. The house is so quiet. It is so empty." She showed us a letter from him.

"'I miss you every day, not just today,'" she read. "This letter is from several months ago. It takes the Red Cross months to get letters out. We can't even communicate with him. How is he going to survive in prison? He's just a boy."

"So far we have been able to visit him twice," Magdi's father added. "Twice in seven months! That is inhumane! On several occasions they gave us permission to visit Magdi, and we made the long trip to the prison, but then the guard simply told us that the permission to see him has been revoked. That is the hardest part. Our hearts are full of hope and excitement that we will see our son, and then they just say no. The ride back home is very sad for all of us. Maybe they treat us this way because I was arrested during the First Intifada."

He held up his right hand, explaining that it been broken by soldiers during the uprising. This was now the second Palestinian I had met who had suffered from broken bones at the hands of Israeli soldiers during the First Intifada. Magdi's father continued.

"Since those three teenagers were kidnapped near Hebron, they've disallowed all visits to prisoners everywhere in Palestine. And that is not the only thing. The conditions have generally gotten worse for the people in prison. Now if you ask for anything from a guard, you automatically get beaten."

I asked Magdi's mother how her younger sons were dealing with their brother's absence. She began to cry.

"At first Yousri would wear Magdi's clothes," she said, pointing to her youngest son, a boy of about eight. "He missed him so much. He still misses him, but it's not as bad as it was at the beginning. He plays a lot of football with his friends, and I thing that makes him forget for a little while." I asked Yousri what position he liked to play.

"Goalkeeper," he said shyly, holding his mother's hand.

"It's what Magdi plays, as well," she explained, beginning to cry once more. "All the men in our family play goalkeeper.

"Going to court is very hard for Magdi. On the court day they force the prisoners to get up early and go to the court together. This means they have to sit through the hearings of all the prisoners, which can take all day. There are bathrooms at the court building, but they don't allow to prisoners to use them, even to urinate. So they have to sit there for eight to ten hours without going to the bathroom. It is a form of torture. Most of them don't drink anything on the day before they are supposed to appear in the court. That way it is not so difficult for them."

Sometimes I envied the inability of Celine and Giselle—two French activists who had arrived in Nablus a few days earlier—to understand Arabic or English, as Abdullah translated most of what was said into English. I knew they comprehended the pain that the family was enduring, but it seemed like they were at least a little removed from it. And when I would tell them the story in French later that evening, they would miss some of its emotional impact.

What saddened me most about this family's story was the image of little Yousri wearing his older brother's clothes. Olivia was crying as we left the house.

"How can these people go on like this?" she asked me. I did not think she was expecting an answer, and I remained silent. There was nothing I could have said, anyway. What choice did the family have? The only thing they could do was go on.

We were silent as we walked back to the center of town to catch a *service* back to Nablus. I wanted to keep thinking about Magdi and his family; I wanted to remember their faces and every aspect of their story. There was nothing I could do to help them, but unlike most of the rest of the world, I had the choice to not ignore them.

29
Thursday, July 24
The Beginning of the Third Intifada?

IN THE MORNING I RECEIVED A PHONE CALL from Cynthia, the media coordinator for ISM in Ramallah. There was to be a huge demonstration at Qalandiya tonight, one of the biggest in years.

"James, there are supposed to be at least 50,000 people there tonight. Try to bring as many from the Nablus team as possible."

Since my arrival in Palestine, I had heard a great deal of talk about an uprising, a so-called "Third Intifada." The kidnapping of the three teenaged settlers had unleashed Operation Brother's Keeper, a military action that had devastating consequences for the population of the West Bank. A number of hate crimes by Jewish Israeli extremists, such as the burning alive of fourteen-year-old Mohamed Abu Khdeir, had resulted in the ire of large segments of the Palestinian population, and there had been demonstrations and clashes in East Jerusalem. The Israeli offensive in Gaza had reached its third week, and Palestinians were exposed to daily reports of atrocities. All of these factors, together with the pent-up frustration at the years of daily humiliations, made some feel that the conditions were ripe for a significant uprising. Perhaps this demonstration was to be the beginning.

By this point, Eve, Johan, Naia, and Sofia had all returned to their native Denmark, but the rest of the team agreed to make the trek to Ramallah to join in the demonstration, which was to take place at nine in the evening. I arrived a few hours early to take part in the financial meeting in my role as ISM's financial coordinator, and the others took a later *service*.

At eight o'clock we all gathered together in the living room of the Ramallah apartment to make preparations. There were roughly twenty of us sitting wherever we could find room: on the couches or on the floor.

As I looked around me, I noted that our group consisted of both Palestinians and internationals from all over the world. There were Italians, British, Danes, Icelanders, Canadians, and Americans. There was even an Israeli woman. The oldest was probably Steve, who appeared to be in his late fifties or early sixties, and the youngest were American students in their early twenties who were studying Arabic at Birzeit University.

Outside of the ISMers from Nablus, I knew roughly half the people in the room, including Silja, a blonde woman in her early twenties from Iceland who was currently the coordinator of the Hebron team. The speaker was Ayman, the young Birzeit student who served both as a medic and ISM's international coordinator.

"This is called the March of the 48,000, but we are hoping there will be many more people there. It's going to be dangerous. I don't want to scare you, but most of you have been here long enough to know what the Israelis are capable of. All the experienced soldiers are in Gaza, and these ones are mostly new recruits. That means they are more dangerous. And they are angry. Israeli soldiers are dying in Gaza, and they want revenge. The commanders know that this demo could be the start of something big, and they want to crush it at all costs. There will be teargas, and there will probably be live ammunition. You are here to support Palestine, and we all appreciate it so much. But now there is real danger. I want you to know there is absolutely no pressure on you to participate in this demo. Nobody will think any less of you if you decide not to go."

I wondered if Ayman was particularly suited to his role as international coordinator simply because of his ability to frighten people. I recalled the training sessions he had given me and Selim upon our arrival in Palestine. His talk about teargas, bullets, arrests, and beatings had made both of us question our decisions to get involved with ISM. And now here I was, weeks later, listening to a similar speech and being frightened once again. The thoughts that I encountered every Friday before the weekly demonstrations at Nabi Saleh, Ni'lin, Bil'in or Kufr Qaddum again spun around in my head. Was there any way I could avoid going to the protest? If I went, could I keep myself safe? In a couple of hours, it would be over, and I would be able to relax. And then, more dramatically, would I die today? And just like always, these questions remained unanswered in my head, and I simply put them aside and decided to go on.

The march was to begin on the road to the Qalandiya checkpoint, one of the many symbols of the Occupation. It is there that most of the Palestinians wishing to enter Israel must line up for hours in long metal cages before being interviewed by Israeli soldiers, who decide whether they are allowed to pass. A procedure I went through once myself, it is arduous and humiliating, and I cannot imagine having to go through it on a daily basis, like many Palestinians do.

In an ideal world, there would be no checkpoint; the marchers would be able to continue along the same road all the way to Jerusalem, although in that case there might not be a reason to protest in the first place. But the checkpoint is there, and that is where the organizers of the march were expecting Israeli soldiers to show up in force to attempt to stop the demonstration.

"The worst of the clashes will be at Qalandiya," Ayman warned. "It's important that some of us be there, right at the front. That's where the action is going to be. We need to organize into groups of three. I will be at the front, so I need two others with me."

There was silence as I looked around the room. Steve, the white-haired man in his fifties who hailed from Birmingham, England, said he would go. Then it was Vitali's turn. Vitali was an Italian ISMer who had shown up in Nablus a week ago. About forty years old, with long blond hair and speaking almost no English, he had left Nablus for Hebron after just a couple of days. I found out later that Vitali had volunteered in Palestine ten years earlier with Vittorio Arrigoni, the Italian ISMer who was kidnapped and subsequently murdered in Gaza in 2011.

The rest of us also broke up into groups of three, half of which would be in the middle of the demonstration while the other half would walk near the end, where the chances of injury were much smaller. I ended up with Celine and Giselle, and together we decided we would spend most of the protest halfway between the front and the back, with the stipulation that we would go forward if circumstances required it.

Abdullah told me he would go to the front, but that he wanted to be by himself. He did not like being responsible for others, and he wanted the freedom to go where he wished.

Ayman's phone rang, and he spoke a few terse words. He smiled.

"It's time to go."

It was by now nine o'clock and darkness had fallen. We walked quickly to al-Manara, Ramallah's central square. There was a great deal of activity in the streets, but I could not tell whether it was more than usual.

I had picked up a kebab before the meeting, and the stall owner had mentioned the demonstration to me, and I overheard another customer talking about it. It seemed like people knew, but would they come?

A block from al-Manara we caught a *service* that took us along the road to Qalandiya. It was the same *service* I had on occasion taken all the way to Jerusalem, but I knew that tonight it would not make it past the checkpoint or even get close to it. After a few minutes the streets began to get progressively more crowded, until finally the crowd was so thick that the *service* could no longer make it through. We disembarked and began to walk.

It was not yet so congested that there was any danger of losing track of one's partners, so we all walked as a group. It was difficult to gauge the mood. It was a mixture of fear, tension, excitement, and celebration. The increasing crowds made me feel like something big was going to happen tonight. There would be danger and some among us would be hurt or possibly even killed, but it felt like the people were rising up.

Part of this feeling arose not just because of the sheer numbers of people, but also from their diversity. It was no longer just about hard-core activists. These were ordinary people. It was in stark contrast to the weekly demonstrations in the villages, where the participants were usually young angry men and older grizzled veterans who seemed like they had been protesting for years, with a few international activists sprinkled in. One almost never saw local women. This was different.

There were both men and women, both old and young. There were still many teenaged boys, but there were also well-dressed businessmen and old women wearing black hijabs. Shop-owners with their sleeves rolled up walked with their wives and held their children by the hand. Walking directly in front of me was a man carrying his daughter on his shoulders. She was wearing a big Palestinian flag as a cape. To her left was a young man with no legs propelling himself forward on a homemade contraption that somehow made locomotion possible. Another man pushed his father in a wheelchair. Motorcycles whizzed through among the marchers. Flags and the traditional Palestinian red-and-white checkered *keffiyehs* dotted the crowd.

The scene reminded me very much of the events at Tahrir Square during the first few days of the Egyptian revolution. I had seen representatives from all sectors of society, and the mood, even though Mubarak had at that point not yet stepped down, had been one of jubilation.

There had also been a sense of cooperation and community. The rich and the poor, and Muslims and Copts all were working together for a common goal: to build a new Egypt. There had been signs showing both the Muslim crescent and the Christian cross. Old grievances could be overlooked in search of a better future. In a particularly poignant moment Christians had stood, arms locked, protecting a group of praying Muslims from the Egyptian security forces.

In Cairo the objective had been clear—to end the Mubarak era and bring democracy to the Egyptian people—but here nobody dared hope for the corresponding goal: to end the Occupation and provide justice for the Palestinians after so many years. In Ramallah tonight, all the marchers wanted was to reach Qalandiya and thereby show the world that they would not be forgotten.

While our side of the street was now filled to the brim with demonstrators, the opposite side was nearly empty, save for ambulances that came screaming through every few minutes, lights flashing, their destination Ramallah's main hospital. It appeared that the clashes had begun at the front. These same ambulances re-appeared shortly thereafter, on our side once more, and the crowd parted as they made their way back towards the front.

After twenty minutes of walking briskly, we found that the crowd had become so dense that it was possible to make further progress only slowly and with difficulty. We had arrived close to the front.

Here the street was illuminated both by the lights in the stores, which had most likely been turned on for this purpose, as well as the flashing lights of the ambulances, of which there were three or four. I did not envy the drivers, who appeared to have great difficulty turning around to deliver their cargo to the hospital. Aiding them were several young men on the street who were running around, desperately trying to create room to allow them to perform this maneuver.

I could tell we were close to the front, because the composition of the crowd had changed. The families had remained in the back, and there were now mostly young men, some of whom were wearing *keffiyehs* to cover their faces. The mood had also changed significantly. Gone were the laughter and the sense of celebration. Faces here were grim and serious.

The area roughly fifty meters in front of us was covered in black smoke, most likely piles of tires lit by the protesters, and it was impossible to see beyond the smoke, except when, every few seconds, flashes of light illuminated the night sky. It was amazing how much the night contributed to the mood at the demonstration. The scene was one of utter confusion. I could not see any soldiers, but it was clear they were there, hidden in the darkness. I did not know whether they were the ones responsible for the flashes of light, or whether it was fireworks set off by demonstrators.

I yelled at a young Palestinian next to me. "Are they using real bullets?" I could not hear his response above the noise, but the answer was clear regardless. Every thirty seconds or so, three or four young men could be seen running from the front, carrying an injured comrade. Like with the Kufr Qaddum shootings that targeted the lower body, I assumed most of the injured had been shot in the leg. The victims kept coming before they were taken to the hospital.

164 THE OTHER SIDE OF THE WALL

I was both impressed and touched by this process, which appeared surprisingly efficient, given the circumstances. I had heard that most of the medics were volunteers, who were risking their lives in this effort. As soon as an ambulance arrived near the front, several young men would direct the crowd to allow the drivers to turn their vehicle around. Another group would clear a path for the victim that would allow him to be carried to the ambulance, which would then speed off for the hospital, only to return a few minutes later to repeat the process.

As I inched towards the front, the smoke and the flashes of light intensified. I could not decide whether I was lucky to be much taller than most of the protesters. On one hand, I did not need to venture as close to the front to get a sense of the action, but on the other I was a more inviting target for Israeli bullets. I knew that a dead Westerner would be a public relations nightmare for the Israelis, and they would most likely not target me directly, but even a stray bullet could have deadly consequences.

I was roughly ten meters from the front when another young man was carried past me, grimacing in pain, his pants stained with blood. My role here was to document the events, not to die in the attempt to do so. I decided to find a different route to the front.

I could see on my right that several fires had been set near the most visible symbol of the Occupation—the Apartheid Wall—which led right up to the checkpoint. This part of the Wall was adorned with a famous portrait of a young Yasser Arafat, as well as British graffiti artist Banksy's most well-known work in Palestine: a small girl lifted in the air by six or seven small balloons. There were a dozen young men here, and the fires cast their shadows eerily onto the Wall as they threw stones at the invisible Israeli soldiers. Above the shadows I could see *No more silent consent or loud indifference* spray painted on the Wall.

There was a house between the street where I was standing and the Wall, and I had to climb a small hill to reach the area between the house and the Wall. The fires there were raging, and I could see now that there were dozens of young men here. Some were throwing stones, while others were merely watching the proceedings. I felt somewhat exposed on the hill, but someone had put up a makeshift wall that consisted of a large piece of aluminum. Roughly two meters by five meters, it was propped up next to the house, but because of the hill it was not flush with the wall of the house; somebody had used what looked like a small metal tray to plug the gap. It was absurd to think that these were the defenses being used to fight off the Israeli army with all of its high-tech weaponry. There were roughly twenty of us crouching behind this contraption, and I wondered whether it could stop an Israeli bullet if a soldier decided to send one in our direction. I would get my answer soon enough.

When I peered above the sheet of aluminum, I saw that the real front was closer to the checkpoint than I had thought. Some sort of barricade—I could not tell whether it was another piece of aluminum or a garbage dumpster—had been placed roughly twenty meters ahead of where the tip of the crowd was.

Behind the barricade were about ten of what I thought must have been incredibly brave young men. Cut off from the main throng of protesters, they were facing the Israeli army by themselves, protected only by a flimsy piece of metal. Ducking behind it, somebody would rise up every few seconds to hurl a stone in the direction of the checkpoint, at the soldiers that were still invisible to me. The smoke was thick in this area, pierced occasionally by lasers emanating from Israeli guns. There were still flashes of light, which I now knew were fireworks set off by the protesters to confuse the soldiers.

I could not imagine being in the small group of young men behind that barricade. When you are in a large group of protesters, you feel somewhat protected. Even when the enemy is out there, trying to harm you, merely looking at the face of the man on your left or right gives you a measure of comfort. It means you are not alone. These men had forsaken this comfort and ventured out by themselves to make this statement against their oppressor. They must have known that they would most likely be shot and possibly even killed.

"James! James!"

It was Abdullah. He was standing just a few meters in front of me, next to the aluminum sheet protecting us. He was waving me forward.

"There is a flight of stairs leading to the roof of the house. We should go up there."

To his left, there was, indeed, a rickety, wooden flight of stairs that was leading somewhere up into the darkness. Lying on the roof, we would be shielded from any potential Israeli fire, and we would have a view of the action down below. But the stairs themselves were above the sheet of aluminum that was protecting us. Was he crazy? It would be a simple matter for any soldier that had the inclination to shoot us there. I inched forward towards the stairs, when I heard it.

PING!

A bullet had hit the piece of aluminum next to us. I will never know whether the soldier who had fired it was trying to hit us and had simply missed, or whether this was a warning shot.

166 THE OTHER SIDE OF THE WALL

When I think about it now, it becomes an important question. The soldiers at Qalandiya were said to be raw and inexperienced, their more accomplished colleagues currently occupied in Gaza. Sometimes I try to imagine being in the boots of that sniper, looking through his gun sight at the young protesters next to the building on the hill. He was probably frightened by the knowledge that there were tens of thousands of angry Arabs on the streets, Arabs who would kill him if they had the chance. If they wanted to kill him, why should he not kill them first? But he was not a killer. He did not want to kill anybody. All he wanted was to go back to his family and his friends. He could see that a few teenagers were trying to climb the stairs and get to the roof of that building. It would be simple to shoot one of them. The rest would run, like they always do. One thing he could count on was his belief that Arabs were cowards. But still, they were people, and it is always wrong to kill. Maybe he should take a single shot at that pathetic piece of aluminum. That would make a lot of noise and scare them.

In fact, on that night the soldier's motivation did not matter to me. I ran, and so did the others around me. We just ran. All I wanted was to get away. Away from the front, the fires, the soldiers, and the bullets, towards the relative safety of the crowd behind us.

I let out a sigh of relief when I realized that I was back in the main throng. Next to me was Olivia, who had somehow been separated from her group. She was crying but clearly relieved to see a familiar face. I realized that she was not hurt, only frightened, like me. Together we walked slowly towards the rear of the demonstration, to find a place where we could take a minute to regroup. We found Nana, a close friend of Olivia's, sitting on the ground, leaning against the side of a building. I left Olivia with her and returned to the front.

Allahu Akbar! Allahu Akbar!

The crowd was now chanting in unison. I had heard this at previous demonstrations. Occasionally when the army's firing reached a particularly high level of intensity, the protesters responded by chanting this phrase repeatedly. It was shouted in a defiant, rather than fearful or pleading tone. The message was not "God help us." It was "God is great! You will never defeat us, no matter how hard you try!"

I could not tell exactly what had happened, but I saw dozens of people running away from the Israeli sniper fire on the roof of the building next to me. I assumed that the soldiers had unleashed an intense barrage in that direction, but I could not be sure.

By now the parade of injured returning from the front had intensified. Every ten seconds somebody was carried towards the rear. Sometimes the victim would be in a horizontal position, in which case he would be supported by five or six men, running towards the closest ambulance. Those whose injuries were less serious would be carried by two men, each of which supported a leg and an arm of the victim, who was sitting more or less upright. Sometimes the face of the injured was visible as he grimaced in pain, and sometimes it would escape from view as he turned it skyward, beseeching his God for help. Usually there was blood, but on occasion there was none, and the exact nature of the injury remained a mystery.

"*Kaam shaheed?*" I heard somebody close to me ask. "How many martyrs?" At demonstrations in Palestine the question is not "How many killed?" Every person who dies at a protest is considered a martyr for the Palestinian cause, and the question is always "How many martyrs?"

"I don't know," was the response. "But there is at least one."

I found out later that there were indeed two martyrs that night, and 287 injured.[1] I did not know whether any Israeli soldiers had been hurt. Steve told me that the person standing next to him at the front had been shot, and that it had looked pretty bad. I wondered if he was one of the ones who had died.

None of the protests I had attended in Palestine had ended abruptly. And so it was with the march at Qalandiya. As the hours wore on, the crowds had dwindled from a high of roughly 20,000[2] to the point where only the serious activists were still protesting. And now even that number was getting smaller. It was time to go home.

Nobody said much as we made our way back to the Ramallah apartment. I thought about the dead and injured, but I was truly grateful to be unhurt and I think most of my friends felt the same way.

After an hour we were back in the apartment. Though I was completely exhausted from the hours at the demonstration, I had no intention of staying the night in the Ramallah apartment. After what I had experienced and witnessed, I longed for the comfort of the familiar, which these days was my mattress back in Nablus. I walked back to al-Manara to catch a *service* back to Nablus. The road was relatively clear, and I was back home in an hour.

Though I was exhausted, I found myself unable to sleep. It felt like the adrenaline was still coursing through my veins and, after tossing and turning for an hour, I gave up and wandered into the living room. It was empty. The entire Nablus team had returned from Ramallah with me, but they were all probably fast asleep.

I knew that it would probably make sleep even harder to come by, but I sat down at the computer to check on the news from Gaza. This time a UN shelter in Beit Hanoun had been hit, resulting in the deaths of sixteen people and more than 200 wounded, most of whom were women and children.[3] A UN spokesman stated that "precise coordinates of the UNRWA shelter had been formally given to the Israeli army" and that the agency had tried twice unsuccessfully to coordinate with the IDF to allow civilians to leave the shelter, but that the IDF had not granted permission. Meanwhile, Israeli officials claimed to have informed people at the shelter to evacuate. An Israeli commander stated that it was still unclear exactly what had happened, but he admitted that "errant fire" by Israeli forces could have been responsible.[4]

I wondered whether this was ever going to stop.

30
Saturday, July 26
Two Murders in Huwarra

AFTER DINNER MY PHONE BUZZED. It was Abdullah. He sounded out of breath.

"Two people were murdered in Huwarra yesterday! We should go find out what happened. Be ready in half an hour. I'll come by and then we can go together."

An hour later, Abdullah, Olivia, Nana, and I were in Huwarra, another village close to Nablus that had a history of confrontation with Israeli settlers and soldiers. Huwarra prides itself on its relative affluence (a villager boasted to us about the high number of German luxury cars in the town), but apparently this wealth was not sufficient to stave off the attacks of the previous day.

There was to be a memorial for the victims in the main mosque, which we were now walking towards. A man in his early forties, wearing a business suit, approached us and whispered a few words to Abdullah. He introduced himself as Mahmoud, shaking our hands heartily. His English was excellent, a fact, he said, that could be attributed to his many travels to the US.

"Today is a very sad day for Huwarra," he told us. "Two people were killed. But please, we will talk about that later. Please come with me."

Mahmoud led us to the mosque, which was one of the largest and best-kept mosques I had seen around Nablus. In front of it was an expansive square filled with mourners, of which there were several hundred. They were sitting in plastic chairs, talking quietly amongst themselves. I assumed they were here to pay their respects to the families of the victims and to listen to the remarks of the local imam, who would be speaking later that evening. We were led to a corner of the square and invited to sit among a small group of old men. We shook hands and sat down, and a boy of about ten served us strong coffee in small paper cups. I saw a young man standing behind one of the chairs looking at us. Mahmoud, noticing my gaze, introduced him.

"This is Yousef," he said. "He is Khalyd's cousin, and he was there when Khalyd was shot."

Mahmoud explained to us that there had been a protest in Huwarra the day before. The townspeople were angry about the massacres taking place in Gaza, and they were marching along the road from the mosque. There were many children, who were walking hand-in-hand with their parents and holding up signs supporting their compatriots in Gaza. It was a peaceful scene, and some of the Israeli soldiers who were watching from their jeeps were taking pictures. But the serenity of the afternoon was shattered when a settler suddenly drove alongside the procession and slammed on his brakes.

The young man standing near our circle said something in Arabic to Mahmoud, who translated for us.

"He was about a meter away from the kids and just started firing out of the window of his car. It was clear that he was trying to kill people."

The settler managed to shoot four people before he drove away. One of them was nineteen-year-old Khalyd Owda, Yousef's cousin, who died from a gunshot wound to the stomach. Three others, including another of cousin of Khalyd's, were injured.

Mahmoud's voice rose as he continued with the story.

"Had he had more ammunition, he would have kept on shooting and killing more people. Killing Palestinians is no big deal for the settlers, because there is no punishment. And what about the soldiers? They were just standing there, doing nothing."

I looked at Yousef as Mahmoud was relating the events of the previous day. His face did not show much emotion; I assumed he was simply too stunned to process what had happened. It was an expression I had seen so many times during the past few weeks. His cousin and good friend had been murdered, and nobody seemed the least bit interested in finding the killer, much less bringing him to justice.

The crowd began to stir.

"Would you like to pay your respects to Khalyd's father?" Mahmoud asked us.

I knew that if I had just lost a close family member, the last thing I would want to do is to talk to strangers, but Mahmoud insisted that talking to us would make him feel that there were people who cared about his son's death.

We joined the long line of people at the front of the square who were waiting to say a few words of encouragement to Khalyd's father and perhaps shake his hand. As the line moved closer, I could see Khalyd's father's face, and I thought of the father of Ahmed Khaled, the handicapped man murdered by the Israeli army in al-Ain refugee camp. Did every father who had lost a young child have the same expression on his face? Both men had suffered a severe blow and were doing all they could just to remain upright. It reminded me of a good friend of mine, who told me on the day his father died that it felt like he had been shot in the stomach with a cannonball.

We approached Khalyd's father. I shook his hand and said, "*Allah yerhamuh.* May God bless him." His blank expression did not change, and I was not even sure that he heard me. I felt awkward and sad, and I just wanted to leave the poor man alone.

Mahmoud led us back to the circle of chairs where we had been sitting previously, and we were once again offered coffee.

Mahmoud proceeded to relate the circumstances surrounding Huwarra's second murder of the day. It was roughly two hours after the settler attack, during clashes between Palestinian youths and Israeli forces. Soldiers were firing teargas, and young men were throwing rocks at them. It was a demonstration much like the ones I had attended so often in the West Bank. During the clashes, an Israeli sniper decided to gun down eighteen-year-old Tayeb Shohada. It was not clear why she chose to do so, since the protesters were reportedly at least a hundred meters away from the soldiers and clearly posed no threat to them. According to witnesses, the sniper shot the victim directly in the eye. Shortly thereafter, her commander was seen to be congratulating her, clapping her on the shoulder. It was neither the first nor the last time that I would hear about Israeli soldiers or settlers expressing joy at the suffering they had inflicted on the local population. It reminded me of children torturing insects with glee.

Medics were unable to reach the victim due to continued Israeli fire. Eventually, he was taken to Rafidia hospital in Nablus, where he was pronounced dead.

***

I found out later that both of the Huwarra victims were students at an-Najah University, where I had been taking Arabic lessons on and off throughout the past few weeks. After class, I would often sit in the main square and watch the students go about their business. Most of the women were veiled, but other than that the scene was reminiscent of the college where I teach in the US. People would be laughing and chatting in groups, or they would be studying quietly, if they had a test coming up or an assignment to hand in. In the summer the heat was oppressive, and usually the students would be sitting on benches in the shade. Perhaps I had seen Khalyd or Tayeb there during one of those afternoons.

Epilogue

A FEW DAYS AFTER THE DEMONSTRATION that was supposed to be the beginning of a Third Intifada and the murders in Huwarra, I left Abdullah and Nablus behind, and I spent the rest of my time in Palestine in Hebron. There I witnessed injustice on an even greater scale than in Nablus.

Hebron is the only Palestinian city in which Israeli settlers and Palestinians live almost literally on top of each other. It has a population of roughly 100,000 inhabitants, who are dominated by a few hundred settlers and the 3,000 soldiers assigned to protect them. Most of these settlers are ideologically motivated and believe their presence in Hebron is justified by religious texts. Their principal goal is to push out the Palestinians, and conflict between the two groups occurs on an almost-daily basis. The ISM apartment in Hebron lies in Tel Rumeida, where the confrontations are particularly common, and my colleagues and I were frequently drawn into them.

There were daily clashes between settlers, soldiers, and Palestinians, with the Palestinians always cast in the role of the victim. We saw soldiers insult a young Palestinian woman walking in front of her house and, when her brother protested, he was arrested and taken away. The next day several Palestinian children, celebrating *Eid*, were blowing bubbles in the street. This offended local settlers, a scuffle ensued, and once again the Palestinians were arrested and taken away. These sorts of incidents take place regularly. In Hebron it is simply part of what passes for normal. Yet some confrontations that summer were particularly fierce. On one occasion there was a demonstration in support of the people of Gaza, and the IDF, using live ammunition, injured close to one hundred protesters.

***

The assault on Gaza continued until late in the summer. A ceasefire between Hamas, Islamic Jihad, and Israel was agreed to on August 26. It began at 7 PM on the following day, bringing to a close seven weeks of fighting.

Both sides claimed victory. There were celebratory parades in Gaza, while Israeli politicians boasted that "Hamas had been dealt a 'devastating blow' with 5,200 'terror sites' targeted and 1,000 'terrorists' killed."[1]

In reality, however, little was achieved, and the terms of the truce were almost identical to those agreed to after the assault on Gaza in 2012. There was little concrete in the agreement, and most of the significant issues—such as the construction of a seaport and an airport in Gaza, the release of Palestinian prisoners, and the disarming of militant groups in Gaza—were left for another day.

The humanitarian consequences of the assault were horrifying, as described by *The Guardian*: "In Gaza more than 2,100 people have been killed, most of them civilians, including about 500 children, in the past seven weeks. At least 11,000 people were injured and more than 17,000 homes destroyed or badly damaged. Around a third of Gaza's 1.8 million people have been displaced, many now living in UN shelters. Schools, hospitals, factories, farms, mosques, and infrastructure such as power and water plants were hit. Reconstruction could take up to ten years, say analysts. On the Israeli side sixty-four soldiers died along with six civilians."[2]

***

After nearly two months in Palestine, I flew out of Tel Aviv on August 11. I was the only passenger in the shuttle from Jerusalem to the airport, and I used the solitude to reflect on my stay in Palestine.

My first few days had taken place a mere seven weeks earlier, but now they seemed almost a lifetime away. They had been frightening at the time, so much so that I had reconsidered my decision to volunteer with ISM. Selim and I had listened as Ayman—standing in front of posters commemorating dead ISMers—lectured us on the various methods the IDF employed to inflict harm on both Palestinians and activists. The fear had never left me—one of the most terrifying nights of my stay occurred in Hebron, quite close to the day of my departure—but it eventually took on a different form. At the beginning it had been a general dread of the unknown that was always with me. Later it evolved into an anxiety that manifested itself only in specific situations, such as at demonstrations or other times of conflict with settlers or soldiers.

Israeli injustice had made its appearance almost immediately after my arrival in Nablus, as soldiers had brutally murdered a mentally handicapped man in a nearby refugee camp. There had been countless victims of Operation Brother's Keeper, the military operation unleashed upon the civilian population in retaliation for the kidnapping of three Israeli settlers. Palestinians had repeatedly been beaten or arrested. Their family members had been murdered, their olive trees cut down, their valuables and money stolen or their homes demolished. Families had seen their sons hauled off to prison. Israeli soldiers had teargassed and shot hundreds of people at Kufr Qaddum, Ni'lin, and Qalandiya.

In early July, the brutality had reached another level altogether, as the IDF had begun its bombing campaign of Gaza, followed shortly thereafter by a ground incursion. Almost every day there had been reports and images of atrocities, as over two thousand people—most of them innocent civilians—had lost their lives.

The most powerful emotion I had experienced was one of rage at the injustice of everything that I had witnessed. There was rage at the Israelis because of their complete disregard for the lives of the Palestinians, rage at my own government for supporting the ongoing injustice, and rage at the world for allowing it to continue.

Yet another overwhelming emotion had been one of complete powerlessness and frustration. Before coming to Palestine I had believed deep down that somehow, by informing people back home about the events that transpired here, I could make them care or, at the very least, that I could make it more difficult for them not to care. I was not sure I had succeeded in that regard. Some of my friends had responded to my stories about the violence and the injustice, but most had seemed unaffected. It was disheartening. A part of me felt dishonest for telling Palestinians that their search for fairness would be aided by my publicizing their experiences. How many times had I given my little speech about the fact that the first step towards justice was making sure that the world was informed about their plight? Once ordinary people knew, I had told them naively, they would pressure their own governments to force the Israeli leadership to act. That was how it was supposed to work. But it seemed that my speech had been an empty one; I had been giving false hope.

And yet I still believed that Palestinians wanted to share their stories with me. I had never coerced them. They had always talked to me willingly, if not enthusiastically. Perhaps part of it had been because of the idea that it might lead to a change in their circumstances, but possibly it was only because they wanted to know that somebody—*anybody*—was paying attention. What they wanted most was to know their suffering was being heard. Perhaps this truly was the most important way in which I could contribute: by listening.

It was important not to give in to the feelings of hopelessness, not to let them overwhelm me. Countless people all over the world cared about the cause of the Palestinians, and they were fighting for justice, whether it was by participating in BDS movements at home or traveling to the West Bank and Gaza to stand in solidarity with the Palestinians and see for themselves the brutality of the Occupation. What message would it send to the Palestinians if the international community did not believe that change was possible? Many of the people I had met in Nablus, Hebron and surrounding villages, who fought and suffered every single day, told me they had felt abandoned by the world. As they continued the battle on the ground, it was incumbent upon international activists to continue fighting abroad.

The conditions in Palestine seemed to be worsening by the day, but there was still cause for cautious optimism among supporters worldwide, whose numbers were growing rapidly. There was a much greater awareness of the actions of the Israeli authorities, as people increasingly received their news, unfiltered, from independent sources instead of the mainstream media. There were protests against the 2014 Israeli assault on Gaza in many of the world's capitals. Opinion polls in the US showed that support for the Palestinians seemed to be increasing, especially among younger voters, whose political power would only increase with time. The BDS movement claimed successes, such as the decision in 2015 by the French corporate giant Veolia to sell off all of its Israeli operations after a vigorous campaign. Despite numerous setbacks—such as the advent of the Trump administration, which has made no secret of its unconditional support for Israel—overall, the international movement on behalf of the Palestinians appeared to be gaining in strength.

The struggle for—as the BDS movement has explicitly stated—freedom, justice and equality for the Palestinians, had to continue unabated, for it was in reality a fight that touched all human beings. As Dr Martin Luther King Jr famously said, "Injustice anywhere is a threat to justice everywhere. We are caught in an inescapable network of mutuality, tied in a single garment of destiny."

Resources

Further Reading

Abunimah, Ali. *The Battle for Justice in Palestine*. Chicago: Haymarket Books, 2014.

Barghouti, Omar. *Boycott, Divestment, Sanctions: The Global Struggle for Palestinian Rights*. Chicago: Haymarket Books, 2011.

Baroud, Ramzy. *Searching Jenin: Eyewitness Accounts of the Israeli Invasion*. Seattle: Cune Press, 2003.

Baroud, Ramzy. *My Father was a Freedom Fighter: Gaza's Untold Story*. London: Pluto Press, 2010.

Blumenthal, Max. *The 51 Day War: Ruin and Resistance in Gaza*. New York: Nation Books, 2015.

Blumenthal, Max. *Life and Loathing in Greater Israel*. New York: Nation Books, 2013.

Carter, Jimmy. *Peace, Not Apartheid*. New York: Simon and Schuster, 2006.

Chomsky, Noam and Pappé, Ilan. *On Palestine*. Chicago: Haymarket Books, 2015.

Dershowitz, Alan. *The Case for Israel*. Hoboken, New Jersey: Wiley, 2003.

Ehrenreich, Ben. *The Way to the Spring: Life and Death in Palestine*. New York: Penguin, 2016.

Falk, Richard. *Palestine's Horizon: Toward a Just Peace*. London: Pluto Press, 2017.

Finkelstein, Norman. *Beyond Chutzpah: On the Misuse of Anti-Semitism and the Abuse of History*. Berkeley and Los Angeles, California: University of California Press, 2005.

Finkelstein, Norman. *The Holocaust Industry: Reflections on the Exploitation of Jewish Suffering (2nd Edition)*. New York: Verso, 2003.

Finkelstein, Norman. *Method and Madness: The Hidden Story of Israel's Assaults on Gaza*. New York and London: OR Books, 2014.

Fisk, Robert. *The Great War for Civilization: The Conquest of the Middle East*. New York: Doubleday, 2007.

Friedman, Thomas. *From Beirut to Jerusalem*. New York: Farrar, Straus & Giroux, 1990.

Gordon, Neve. *Israel's Occupation*. Berkeley: University of California Press, 2008.

Halper, Jeff. *War Against the People: Israel, Palestine and Global Pacification*. London: Pluto Press, 2015.

Hammond, Jeremy. *Obstacle to Peace: The US Role in the Israeli-Palestinian Conflict*. Cross Village, Michigan: Worldview Publications, 2016.

Hirst, David. *The Gun and the Olive Branch: The roots of violence in the Middle East*. New York: Thunder Mouth Press: Nation Books, 2003.

Khalidi, Rashid. *The Iron Cage: The Story of the Palestinian Struggle for Statehood*. Boston: Beacon Press, 2006.

Mearsheimer, John and Walt, Stephen. *The Israeli Lobby and US Foreign Policy*. New York: Farrar, Straus & Giroux, 2007.

Olson, Pamela. *Fast Times in Palestine: A Love Affair with a Homeless Homeland*. Berkeley: Seal Press, 2013.

Pappé, Ilan. *The Ethnic Cleansing of Palestine*. London: Oneworld Publications, 2006.

Pappé, Ilan. *The Idea of Israel: A History of Power and Knowledge*. New York: Verso, 2014.

Peled, Miko. *The General's Son: Journey of an Israeli in Palestine (2nd Edition)*. Charlottesville, Virginia: Just World Books, 2016.

Rothchild, Alice. *Condition Critical: Life and Death in Israel/Palestine*. Charlottesville, Virginia: Just World Books, 2017.

Shlaim, Avi. *The Iron Wall: Israel and the Arab World (Updated and Expanded)*. New York and London: Norton, 2014.

Weir, Alison. *Against Our Better Judgment: The Hidden History of How the U.S. Was Used to Create Israel*. Self-published, 2014.

White, Ben. *The 2014 Gaza War: 21 Questions and Answers*. Self-published, 2016.

Notes

For the Notes please see http://richardhardigan.com/osw/endnotes/

Acknowledgments

I would like to express my gratitude to the many people without whom this book never would have been written:

To my mother and sister, who always believed that I could do something so far out of my comfort zone.

To Abdullah, my friend who shared so much of his life with me and who showed me the ropes in Palestine.

To Scott C. Davis of Cune Press, for taking a chance on a scientist trying his hand at non-academic writing for the first time.

To Diep Vuong and Toan Nguyen, the production crew at Cune Press, for their attention to detail.

To George, for doing an amazing editing job on a manuscript that was far from publishable when I first gave it to him.

To Selim, Peter, Silja and all the other ISMers that I met in 2014, for having my back in all those hairy situations in the West Bank.

To my incredible wife, who read and corrected parts of all those early versions of the book, and most importantly, whose support for me never wavered.

Index

CUNE PRESS WAS FOUNDED in 1994 to publish thoughtful writing of public importance. Our name is derived from "cuneiform." (In Latin *cuni* means "wedge.")

In the ancient Near East the development of cuneiform script—simpler and more adaptable than hieroglyphics—enabled a large class of merchants and landowners to become literate. Clay tablets inscribed with wedge-shaped stylus marks made possible a broad intermeshing of individual efforts in trade and commerce.

Cuneiform enabled scholarship to exist, art to flower, and created what historians define as the world's first civilization. When the Phoenicians developed their sound-based alphabet, they expressed it in cuneiform.

The idea of Cune Press is the democratization of learning, the faith that rarefied ideas—pulled from dusty pedestals and displayed in the streets—can transform the lives of ordinary people. And it is the conviction that ordinary people, trusted with the most precious gifts of civilization, will give our culture elasticity and depth—a necessity if we are to survive in a time of rapid change.

 Aswat: Voices from a Small Planet (a series from Cune Press)

Looking Both Ways	Pauline Kaldas
Stage Warriors	Sarah Imes Borden
Stories My Father Told Me	Helen Zughraib
The Iron Butterfly	Marream Krollos

 Syria Crossroads (a series from Cune Press)

Leaving Syria	Bill Dienst & Madi Williamson
Visit the Old City of Aleppo	Khaldoun Fansa
The Plain of Dead Cities	Bruce McLaren
Steel & Silk	Sami Moubayed
Syria - A Decade of Lost Chances	Carsten Wieland
The Road from Damascus	Scott C. Davis
The Dusk Visitor	Musa Al-Halool
A Pen of Damascus Steel	Ali Ferzat
White Carnations	Musa Rahum Abbas
East of the Grand Umayyad	Sami Moubayed

 Bridge Between the Cultures (a series from Cune Press)

Congo	Frederic Hunter
Turning Fear Into Power	Linda Sartor
Apartheid is a Crime	Mats Svensson
A Year at the Edge of the Jungle	Frederic Hunter
The Girl Ran Away	Frederic Hunter

 Cune   Cune Press: www.cunepress.com / cunepress.info

Richard Hardigan is a university professor living in the United States. Between 2006 and 2015 he spent a total of four years living and working in the Middle East.

While teaching in Egypt, the author was caught up in the Tahrir Square uprising of January, 2011, an experience that shaped his views on the value and effectiveness of peaceful protest. He spent the summer of 2013 in Palestine working on his Arabic, and while traveling throughout the country he was shocked at the ubiquitous injustice he witnessed. The following summer he returned to Palestine and volunteered with the International Solidarity Movement for two months, where he acted in solidarity with the Palestinians in their resistance against the brutal Israeli occupation. It is this experience that he describes in *The Other Side of the Wall*. In 2015 he lived in and reported from the Palestinian refugee camp of Shatila in Lebanon, site of the massacre of 1982.

The author has written extensively about his experiences in Palestine and Lebanon. His work can be found at http://www.richardhardigan.com.